Citizens of the Kingdom

By Matthew Allen

© 2025 Spiritbuilding Publishers.

All rights reserved. No part of this book may be reproduced without the publisher's written permission.

Published by
Spiritbuilding Publishers
9700 Ferry Road, Waynesville, OH 45068

CITIZENS OF THE KINGDOM
By Matthew Allen

ISBN: 978-1-964-80543-6

Spiritbuilding
PUBLISHERS

spiritbuilding.com

Table of Contents

Preface 1
Introduction 2
How to Use This Workbook 4

Part 1   **The King and His Authority** 7
Lesson 1   The Rights of the King 8
Lesson 2   Our King Is Like No Other 16

Part 2   **The Heart of a Servant** 23
Lesson 3   Servants By Choice 24
Lesson 4   Daily Life in the Kingdom 30
Lesson 5   The King's Job Plan 36

Part 3   **Listening and Obeying** 43
Lesson 6   Citizens Listen to the King 44
Lesson 7   Three Attitudes Kingdom Citizens Must Avoid 50
Lesson 8   Kingdom Citizens Focus on Heaven 56

Part 4   **Our Identity and Mission** 63
Lesson 9   What It Means to Be a Citizen 64
Lesson 10   Forgiveness in the Kingdom 70
Lesson 11   Ambassadors of the Kingdom 75

Part 5   **Faithful Until He Comes** 81
Lesson 12   Kingdom Stewardship:
                  Using Our Gifts for God's Glory 82
Lesson 13   Until the King Comes:
                  Holding Fast in the Kingdom 87

Preface

The Kingdom of God is the reign of Christ over every heart that surrenders to Him, and it is the hope of a future where His rule will be fully revealed. This workbook is built on one simple truth: **the Kingdom is everything.**

Too often, Christians think of the Kingdom as something far off, something that begins when we die or when Jesus returns. But the New Testament paints a different picture. The Kingdom is already here. Jesus inaugurated it with His life, death, and resurrection. And now, He calls us to live as citizens of that Kingdom, *right now, in this world.*

This study is not about theory. It's about transformation. Each lesson is designed to help you think seriously and personally about what it means to live under the reign of King Jesus. It's about surrendering your rights, aligning your life with the King's will, and embracing your role as a citizen in His eternal Kingdom.

In *Citizens of the Kingdom,* we will examine the rights and authority of the King, our identity as citizens, the mission we've been given, and the hope that sustains us. These studies are based on Scripture and are intended to be practical, convicting, and straightforward.

Whether you are using this workbook in a Bible class, small group, or personal study, I pray it will challenge you to examine your priorities, deepen your loyalty to Jesus, and live with confidence that the Kingdom you belong to cannot be shaken.

Long live the King.

Matthew Allen

June 2025

Introduction

What does it really mean to belong to the Kingdom of God?

This question lies at the core of everything Jesus taught. The Kingdom of God was not a secondary theme; it was the main message of His ministry. From the very beginning, Jesus proclaimed, *"The time is fulfilled, and the kingdom of God has come near. Repent and believe the good news"* (Mark 1:15).

He spoke in parables to describe it (Matthew 13). He healed to demonstrate its power (Matthew 12:28). He welcomed the poor, the broken, and the outcast, showing that the Kingdom is for those who recognize their need for grace. And He taught His followers to pray, *"Your kingdom come. Your will be done on earth as it is in heaven"* (Matthew 6:10).

But for many Christians today, the Kingdom has been seen as something vague or only about the future, something we'll experience "someday." That's not how Jesus described it. The Kingdom is not just a future reward; it is a current reality. It's not solely about going to heaven when we die, but about living under the reign of King Jesus **right now**.

In **Colossians 1:13**, Paul reminds us that God *"has rescued us from the domain of darkness and transferred us into the kingdom of the Son He loves."* The Kingdom isn't something we're waiting to enter; it's something we've already been brought into by God's grace. As citizens of this Kingdom, we are called to live differently, shaped by the values, priorities, and mission of our King.

That's what this workbook is about.

Over thirteen lessons, we will explore what it means to live as citizens of the Kingdom. We will study the rights and authority of our King. We will examine the life He calls us to live. We'll consider how we serve, speak, forgive, suffer, and endure as those under Christ's rule. We'll discuss identity, obedience, stewardship, and purpose. And we'll be prompted to ask: *Are we truly living like the Kingdom is everything*?

These lessons are based on Scripture. They are meant to be clear, practical, and inspiring thought. Whether you use this book in a Bible class, small group, or personal study, I hope it helps you see the Kingdom not as an abstract idea but as your current reality and your highest calling.

Jesus said, *"Seek first the kingdom of God and His righteousness, and all these things will be provided for you"* (Matthew 6:33). That's the goal of this study: to help you seek the Kingdom first, surrender every part of your life to the King, and prepare you to stand firm, serve boldly, and shine brightly until He returns.

Because the Kingdom is not just near.

It's here.

And the King is worthy of everything.

How to Use This Workbook

This workbook is designed to guide you through thirteen focused lessons on the life, priorities, and mission of a Kingdom citizen. Each lesson is centered on Scripture and built to help you reflect, respond, and grow in your walk with the King.

Here's how the workbook is structured:

Summary Scripture

Each lesson begins with a key verse or passage that captures the heart of the theme. You are encouraged to read it aloud, memorize it, or reflect on it throughout the week.

Introduction

This section sets the stage for the lesson. It explains why the topic matters and how it connects to life in the Kingdom of God.

Main Points (1–3)

Each lesson includes three fully developed teaching points. These provide biblical insight, real-life application, and reflection prompts to help you personally engage with the material. Teachers can use these points as the foundation for group discussion or class instruction.

Application

This section is written as a pastoral challenge. It calls for honest self-examination and helps drive home the "so what" of the lesson.

Summary and Conclusion

Each lesson ends with a closing paragraph that reinforces the big ideas and offers encouragement to stay faithful to the King.

Discussion & Reflection Questions

Five workbook-style questions are provided at the end of each lesson. These are great for personal journaling or for use in a group setting. They aim to move the truth from your head to your heart, and into your life.

Ways You Can Use This Workbook:

- **Bible Classes:** Each lesson is ideal for a weekly group setting. Teachers can use the teaching points, questions, and Scripture readings to guide a 30–45 minute class.
- **Small Groups:** The workbook can also be used in home studies or men's/women's groups. The reflection questions make for rich spiritual conversation.
- **Personal Study:** If you're working through this on your own, take time with each section. Read the Scriptures slowly. Use the margins and lines to write your thoughts and prayers.
- **Family Devotionals:** These lessons are written plainly and are easy to adapt for teens or families. Discuss a few key points around the table and talk about how to live them out together.

Final Note

You won't get the most out of this study by rushing through it. Slow down. Reflect. Wrestle with what it means to live under the reign of Christ. These truths are meant to be lived, not just learned.

And remember: the goal of this workbook isn't just to fill in pages. It's to help you live fully for the King.

PART ONE

The King and His Authority

Lesson 1

The Rights of the King

For this reason God highly exalted him and gave him the name that is above every name, so that at the name of Jesus every knee will bow— in heaven and on earth and under the earth— and every tongue will confess that Jesus Christ is Lord, to the glory of God the Father, Philippians 2:9–11

Introduction

We don't often think about what it means to live under a king's rule. In America, we grow up with the idea of personal freedom and independence. We vote for our leaders. We challenge authority. We cherish individual rights. But in the Kingdom of God, things are different. Jesus isn't elected. His authority isn't up for debate. He reigns by divine right because He is the Son of God.

The Bible teaches that one day, *"every knee will bow … and every tongue will confess that Jesus Christ is Lord"* (Philippians 2:10–11). This is not just a suggestion. It's a fact. Jesus has been given all authority in heaven and on earth (Matthew 28:18). Whether we bow in joyful submission or face final judgment, we will all acknowledge Him as King.

But Jesus is unlike the tyrants of history. He is neither cruel nor self-serving. He is *the Prince of Peace*, the *Wonderful Counselor*, the *Everlasting Father*[1] (Isaiah 9:6). His rule brings blessings, not bondage. His commands are not burdensome; they lead to life. He is the type of King who gives everything for His people, including His own life.

This lesson begins at the foundation of the entire series: **Jesus has the right to rule.** He created us. He redeemed us. He sustains us. And as citizens in His Kingdom, we must surrender completely to His authority.

---

1   Everlasting Father here means "Father of Eternity," a royal, fatherly ruler, without collapsing the Persons of the Trinity.

The King Was Promised

Long before Jesus was born, God promised a King. The Old Testament is full of prophecies about a coming ruler who would rule with justice, bring peace, and have authority over all nations. These promises weren't vague guesses. They were clear statements pointing to Jesus.

Genesis 49:10

"The scepter will not depart from Judah or the staff from between his feet until he whose right it is comes and the obedience of the peoples belongs to him."

Jacob spoke these words about one of his sons, Judah. This was the first clear sign that God's chosen King would come from Judah's family line. The "scepter" is a symbol of kingship. And this King would not rule just over Israel, but over all people.

2 Samuel 7:12–16

"Your house and kingdom will endure before me forever, and your throne will be established forever."

God made this promise to King David. While David's son Solomon was to sit on the throne next, God was signaling beyond him. He was promising an **eternal King**, one who would rule forever. This was ultimately fulfilled in Jesus, who is called the "Son of David" and now reigns forever at God's right hand.

Psalm 2

This psalm describes a King anointed by God, one who rules over the nations and receives the ends of the earth as His possession. The early Christians applied this directly to Jesus (see Acts 4:25–27). It is one of the clearest "royal" psalms pointing forward to the authority and power of Christ.

Zechariah 9:9–10

"Rejoice greatly, Daughter Zion! Shout in triumph, Daughter Jerusalem! Look, your King is coming to you; he is righteous and victorious, humble and riding on a donkey, on a colt, the foal of a donkey. ... He will declare peace to the nations." Jesus fulfilled this prophecy exactly when He entered Jerusalem the week of His death (Matthew 21:5). He came not with armies and force, but with gentleness and humility. Yet His reign would reach to the ends of the earth.

The coming of Jesus was no accident. The prophets pointed to Him repeatedly. His birth, life, and rule were all part of God's plan. The King was promised. The King has come. And He still reigns today.

The King Now Reigns

Jesus is not waiting to become King. He already is. His reign began when He rose from the dead and ascended to the right hand of God. From that moment forward, He has held all authority in heaven and on earth. He is not just our future hope, He is our present King.

Matthew 28:18

"All authority in heaven and on earth has been given to me."

This is a direct statement of Jesus' power. There is no higher court. No stronger ruler. No shared power. When Jesus rose from the dead, He was exalted to the highest place. He didn't gain some authority—He was given *all* of it.

Ephesians 1:20–22

God "raised him from the dead and seated him at his right hand... far above all rule and authority and power and dominion... and put all things under his feet."

This is the fulfillment of God's promise to David in 2 Samuel 7. Jesus now sits on the throne. He reigns above every earthly government, every spiritual power, and every human life. Nothing is outside His rule, not even death.

Colossians 3:1

"Christ is seated at the right hand of God."

This is where He is right now. Ruling. Reigning and interceding for His people. He is not passive. He is not distant. He is actively leading His church and directing history toward its final outcome.

John 18:36

"My kingdom is not of this world."

Jesus clearly told Pilate that He wasn't competing for a worldly throne. His rule isn't connected to borders or political systems. His Kingdom is spiritual and everlasting. It follows different values and standards.

Revelation 19:16

"On His robe and on His thigh He has a name written, King of kings and Lord of lords."

This is the final picture of Jesus in Scripture, not suffering, not buried, but riding in victory as the undisputed King. He has no rival. His name is above every name. And He is coming again to bring judgment and reward.

Jesus is not just a part of your life; He rules your life. As citizens of His Kingdom, we live under His authority every day. We don't give Him part of our heart. We give Him everything.

What This Means for Us

If Jesus is King, then we are not in control. That's the core issue. We don't negotiate with Him or choose which commands to follow. He has the authority to govern every part of our lives: our thoughts, choices, relationships, and priorities. This is what true discipleship means: complete surrender to the King.

He Rules Our Life

"I have been crucified with Christ, and I no longer live, but Christ lives in me. The life I now live in the body, I live by faith in the Son of God, who loved me and gave himself for me," Galatians 2:20.

Following Jesus means we give up control. His will becomes our will. His way becomes our way. He doesn't share the throne with us; we step off so He can reign.

He Owns Us

"You were bought at a price; do not become slaves of people," 1 Corinthians 7:23.

We belong to Jesus. We don't just worship Him, we serve Him. His blood paid for us. That changes everything about how we live.

He Commands Obedience

"Now if we died with Christ, we believe that we will also live with him," Romans 6:8.

"...present yourselves to God as those who are alive from the dead, and your members to God as weapons for righteousness," Romans 6:13.

Being in the Kingdom means we no longer live for sin. Our bodies, our time, and our energy are now for the King's use.

He Gives Strength and Victory

"Therefore, let us approach the throne of grace with boldness, so that we may receive mercy and find grace to help us in time of need," Hebrews 4:16.

"Thanks be to God, who gives us the victory through our Lord Jesus Christ!" 1 Corinthians 15:57.

Because He rules, we can face anything. Trials don't shake us. Death doesn't defeat us. Our King is on the throne, and He fights for us.

Jesus isn't asking for a place in your life. He demands the whole thing. But in surrendering to Him, we find true freedom, purpose, and peace.

Application: Living Under the Rule of the King

If Jesus truly reigns as King, then our whole life must reflect that truth. It's not enough to agree with His authority; we must respond with full surrender. A king doesn't seek suggestions… he issues commands. Our King, Jesus, is not only deserving of obedience; He is also loving, wise, and just. Submitting to Him brings peace and purpose. So, how does that submission appear in everyday life?

First, *it means giving up control*. Most people want to make their own choices. We like the idea of Jesus as Savior, but we resist Him as King. However, you cannot have one without the other. If Jesus has all authority in heaven and on earth, then our plans, goals, and decisions must align with His will. We must ask not just, "What do I want to do?" but, "What does my King command me to do?" This includes how we treat others, how we manage our finances, how we resolve conflicts, and what we value most. His authority is not limited to spiritual matters, it extends into every part of our lives.

Second, *we must treat His word as final*. In our culture, truth is often seen as flexible. But the citizen of the Kingdom listens carefully to the words of the King and obeys them without twisting to fit personal preferences. When Jesus speaks, we don't edit. We don't delay. We respond in faith. His teachings are not suggestions—they are the foundation of our life. Whether we're reading the Sermon on the Mount, hearing His parables, or studying His commands through the apostles, our posture must always be one of reverence and obedience.

Third, *our loyalty to the King should be evident both publicly and privately*. Many people seem faithful at church but live as if they're in charge the rest of the week. True allegiance is consistent. It appears in our work ethic, how we speak to family members, and how we handle temptation when no one is watching. Loyalty means we don't hide who we serve. We openly live for Christ, showing others our devotion and hopefully drawing them to Him through our example.

Finally, *living under the rule of the King means we stop negotiating with Him*. We all have areas we'd rather keep to ourselves: certain habits, relationships, or ambitions that we hesitate to give up. But Jesus doesn't reign over just part of us. He claims all of us. He calls us to take up our cross daily and follow Him with full devotion. That doesn't mean we'll be perfect, but it does mean we stop making excuses and start making changes. Every day offers a new opportunity to renew our surrender.

If there's one area of your life you've been holding back from the King, now is the time to let it go. Write it down. Pray over it. Then take one clear, specific action this week to fully surrender that part of your life to Jesus. He is worthy of that ... and more.

Conclusion

The Kingdom of God operates differently from the kingdoms of men. In this Kingdom, there is only one rightful ruler: Jesus Christ. He is not King because we chose Him, but because God exalted Him. His kingship is based on creation, validated through prophecy, and affirmed by His resurrection and ascension. He is currently seated at the right hand of God, reigning with full authority in heaven and on earth. One day, every knee will bow and every tongue will confess that He is Lord.

But for now, we have a choice. We can submit willingly, or we can resist His rule and try to build our own kingdom. One leads to life; the other leads to ruin. Jesus is not a passive figurehead—He is the risen, reigning King of kings. He demands our loyalty, obedience, and trust. He doesn't want to be part of your life; He wants all of it.

If you claim to follow Christ, then He must govern your heart, habits, thoughts, and direction. Every decision you make should show that your life no longer belongs to you—it belongs to the King. And this is not a burden; it is our joy. Because our King is good, merciful, just, and He has given everything for His people.

So, the question is simple: **Is Jesus truly your King? Or are you still trying to sit on the throne?** This lesson calls you to surrender: to step down, lay aside your rights, and give Jesus what He deserves: complete authority over your life.

For Discussion

Use the space below to reflect on Jesus' kingship and authority.

1. Why do you think modern people, even Christians, often struggle with the idea of Jesus having absolute authority over their lives? *What are some areas where this resistance shows up today?*

_____
_____
_____

2. How does the concept of kingship in Scripture differ from our cultural understanding of leadership or power? *What does that teach us about how we view Jesus?*

_____
_____
_____

3. Jesus reigns now, not just in the future. How should that truth affect the way you make daily decisions? *Can you name a recent decision that reflected (or resisted) His rule?*

_____
_____
_____

4. Which part of your life is hardest to fully surrender to King Jesus, and why? *What fears, habits, or beliefs make it hard to submit?*

_____
_____
_____

5. When we submit to Jesus as King, what blessings or freedoms come with that surrender? *How have you personally experienced His rule as a source of peace or stability?*

_____
_____
_____

Lesson 2

Our King Is Like No Other

Adopt the same attitude as that of Christ Jesus, who, existing in the form of God, did not consider equality with God as something to be exploited. Instead he emptied himself by assuming the form of a servant, taking on the likeness of humanity. And when he had come as a man, he humbled himself by becoming obedient to the point of death— even to death on a cross,
Philippians 2:5–8

Introduction

We don't expect kings to serve. Kings take. They demand loyalty, collect taxes, and exercise control. In the world we know, power often leads to pride, and those in charge tend to make life easier for themselves, not harder. That's why the reign of Jesus is so shocking. He does the opposite.

Jesus didn't come to be served, but to serve. And not just in small, symbolic ways. He gave up His position, His comfort, and ultimately His life to lift others up. He didn't use His power to escape suffering; He used it to walk into suffering on our behalf. His throne was a cross. His crown was made of thorns. His mission was to die for the people who rejected Him.

Jesus said: "For even the Son of Man did not come to be served, but to serve, and to give his life as a ransom for many," Mark 10:45.

That one verse separates Jesus from every ruler the world has ever known. He calls His followers to live with that same humility. In His Kingdom, greatness comes through service. Authority is used to bless, not to boast. Leadership means sacrifice, not status.

Jesus is a King, but not the kind we expect. He is a King like no other.

True Greatness Looks Like Service

Mark 10:35–45 shows us Jesus walking toward His death. He just told His disciples that He would be mocked, flogged, killed, and raised again.

But right after this serious moment, James and John pulled Him aside with a request.

"Allow us to sit at your right and at your left in your glory," (v. 37). They still didn't understand what kind of King Jesus was. They were focused on status, power, and position. But Jesus was focused on a cross. He asked them if they could drink the cup He was about to drink, meaning, *could they suffer with Him?* They said yes, not realizing what they were agreeing to. The other disciples were angry, but probably for selfish reasons; they likely wanted those spots too.

Jesus didn't rebuke them harshly. He corrected them gently but firmly. He said: "You know that those who are regarded as rulers of the Gentiles lord it over them … But it is not so among you. On the contrary, whoever wants to become great among you will be your servant." (vv. 42–43). And then He gave the ultimate reason why. Mark 10:45 flips the world's definition of greatness. In His Kingdom, the highest place belongs to the lowest servant. Greatness isn't about being in charge; it's about giving yourself away. Leadership isn't about honor; it's about sacrifice.

This is what makes Jesus a King like no other. He didn't demand to be served. He became the servant. He didn't seek His own comfort. He laid it down. He didn't ask others to suffer for Him. He suffered for them. And in doing so, He showed us what true greatness looks like.

How would your daily life change if you truly believed that greatness in God's Kingdom is measured by humility, not recognition?

Our King Gave His Life for His People

Jesus came to "give his life as a ransom for many," Mark 10:45.

This is one of the clearest and most powerful statements Jesus ever made about His mission.

Most kings send others into battle to die for them. But Jesus did the opposite. He came to earth to lay down His life for sinners, enemies, and the undeserving. The word "ransom" means a price paid to free someone from captivity. Jesus saw us enslaved to sin and death, and He chose to become the payment that would set us free.

This wasn't just a moment of compassion; it was the King's plan from the start. The entire mission of Jesus was centered on this sacrifice. He came to serve and to save. He didn't cling to His rights or demand honor. He gave Himself completely.

Isaiah 53 had already prophesied that the Messiah would be "despised and rejected," "pierced because of our rebellion," and that "the punishment for our peace was on him" (Isaiah 53:3–5). Jesus fulfilled that prophecy in full. He bore our sin. He carried our guilt. He suffered the punishment that should have fallen on us.

And this wasn't forced on Him. He said in John 10:18: "No one takes it from me, but I lay it down on my own." This is the heart of the gospel. The King didn't come to dominate but to deliver. He didn't cling to power but surrendered to the cross. And that's what makes Him unlike any ruler the world has ever seen.

When you think of Jesus as King, do you picture a throne, or a cross? How does His sacrifice shape the way you respond to His authority?

Our King Calls Us to Follow His Example

"You call me Teacher and Lord—and you are speaking rightly, since that is what I am. So if I, your Lord and Teacher, have washed your feet, you also ought to wash one another's feet. For I have given you an example, that you also should do just as I have done for you," John 13:13–15.

On the night before His death, Jesus did something nobody expected. He got up from the table, wrapped a towel around His waist, and started washing His disciples' feet. This was usually the job of a servant, something most people would have considered beneath them. But Jesus did it intentionally. Then He looked at them and said: *"I have given you an example."*

This is the way of life in the Kingdom. Jesus doesn't just ask us to admire His humility; He commands us to imitate it. We are called to humble ourselves, serve others, set aside pride, and live for more than just our own comfort. If the King was willing to serve in this manner, how can His followers live any differently?

This call to imitation runs throughout the New Testament:
- **Philippians 2:5** says, "Adopt the same attitude as that of Christ Jesus."
- **1 Peter 2:21** says, "You were called to this, because Christ also suffered for you, leaving you an example, that you should follow in his steps."

This is how greatness in the Kingdom is measured: not by how many people serve us, but by how many we're willing to serve. Not by how high we rise, but by how low we're willing to go. Jesus didn't just die to save us; He lived to show us how to live. The more we understand what kind of King He is, the more we'll want to follow His example, not just in belief, but in action.

Are there ways you try to hold on to position, recognition, or comfort instead of taking the posture of a servant? What would it look like to wash someone's feet this week, not literally, but through humble service?

Application: Becoming Like the King Who Serves

The lesson of Jesus' kingship is deeply personal. *It demands a response.* If Jesus truly is a King like no other, then our lives should reflect that through how we treat others, use our influence, and view greatness. In the Kingdom of God, power isn't a tool for control; it's a platform for service. Jesus used His authority to uplift others, and now He calls us to do the same.

This involves *putting aside selfish ambition*. Like the disciples, we can easily get caught up in seeking recognition, status, or comfort. But Jesus told them, and us, that greatness is not about being first, but about being last. It's not about climbing higher, but about going lower. We must learn to adopt the posture of a servant in our homes, congregations, and communities.

Following Jesus's example involves *letting go of the need to always be right, always be heard, or always receive credit*. It means seeking ways to bless those who cannot repay us, listening to the overlooked, and quietly stepping in to do the work no one else wants to do. True greatness appears in small acts of kindness, silent sacrifices, and patient endurance.

And more than anything, *it means remembering that our King sacrificed His life for us.* His service wasn't temporary or convenient … it cost Him everything. He carried our sin, bore our shame, and died to bring us into His Kingdom. Ask yourself honestly: Where do I need to stop pursuing status and start offering service? Who around me needs help, encouragement, or care, and what's holding me back from giving it?

Jesus is not just a King to be admired. He is a King to be followed. The more we walk in His steps, the more His Kingdom will shine through our lives.

Conclusion

Jesus redefined what it means to be a King. He had every right to demand service, recognition, and comfort. Instead, He humbled Himself to serve, chose suffering over safety, and gave His life for those who didn't deserve it. No other ruler has done that. No other king has that kind of heart.

He taught His followers that true greatness comes through humility, not power. He demonstrated that leadership involves sacrifice. And He calls us to live that way as well. His words in Mark 10:45 are a call to action: "For even the Son of Man did not come to be served, but to serve, and to give his life as a ransom for many."

This is the King we follow. This is the Kingdom we belong to.

So now we must ask: Are we trying to follow Jesus while still clinging to the world's view of greatness? Are we seeking comfort instead of sacrifice, attention instead of service?

If Jesus is truly our King, then we must learn to love what He loved, do what He did, and serve how He served. That's what it means to belong to a King like no other.

For Discussion

Use the space below to think about what it means to serve.

1. Why do you think the disciples were so focused on position and recognition in Mark 10? *How does this mindset show up in our lives today?*

_____
_____
_____

2. Mark 10:45 says Jesus gave His life "as a ransom for many." *What does that mean to you personally?*

_____
_____
_____

3. Jesus washed His disciples' feet as an example. *What are some modern, everyday ways we can "wash feet" in our homes, churches, or communities?*

_____
_____
_____

4. Where in your life do you find it hardest to take the posture of a servant? *What's holding you back?*

_____
_____
_____

5. How can the humility of King Jesus shape the way you treat others this week? *Be specific.*

_____
_____
_____

Part Two

The Heart of a Servant

Lesson 3

Servants By Choice

But thank God that, although you used to be slaves of sin, you obeyed from the heart that pattern of teaching to which you were handed over, and having been set free from sin, you became enslaved to righteousness,
Romans 6:17–18.

Introduction

What motivates someone to serve a king? In many kingdoms, people serve because they feel compelled to. They obey out of fear. Their loyalty is driven by the fear of punishment or a desire to maintain their status. But in the Kingdom of Christ, the foundation is entirely different. Jesus doesn't force anyone to follow Him. He invites. He calls. And those who choose to follow Him do so willingly, not because they are pressured, but out of deep love and gratitude.

This is what makes the Kingdom of God so special. Jesus isn't a tyrant. He doesn't rule through intimidation or demand service out of fear. Instead, He governs through grace and sacrifice. Because of that, the only proper response is voluntary surrender. We serve Him not because we have to, but because we want to. We trust Him. We love Him. And we know that no one else is deserving of our life and loyalty.

But surrender doesn't come easily. Our culture constantly encourages us to stay in control, make our own choices, and chase our dreams. Giving in to someone else, even Jesus, can feel like a loss. But it's not. Surrendering to Christ is the only way to find true freedom. When we give up the throne of our hearts, Jesus takes His rightful place, and our lives begin to align under His rule.

This lesson explores what it means to become a servant by choice. We will see that our King desires a committed people and calls us to serve not out of guilt, but with joy.

Our King Has the Right to Rule Our Lives

One of the clearest messages in Scripture is that Jesus Christ has complete authority over our lives. He is not just our Savior; He is our **Lord**. That means He has the right to govern. And because of who He is and what He has done, we willingly give Him that position.

Colossians 1:16–18 states: "For everything was created by him, in heaven and on earth, the visible and the invisible... all things have been created through him and for him. He is before all things, and by him all things hold together... so that he might come to have first place in everything." This forms the foundation of Christian service. We serve Jesus because He is the **Creator**, the **Sustainer**, and the **Head of the church**. Without Him, we wouldn't exist. Because of Him, we've been redeemed. And now, because of His rightful rule, we surrender everything to Him. We no longer call the shots. He does.

The Scriptures speak plainly:

- Jesus now reigns at the right hand of God (Romans 8:34; Ephesians 1:20–22; Hebrews 1:13).
- His rule is not partial, it's total. There is no one higher.
- We were bought at a price, the price of His blood (1 Corinthians 7:23; 1 Peter 1:19).

But this kind of rule isn't strict or controlling. Jesus doesn't lead us with fear. He doesn't use guilt or intimidation. He guides us through His love, grace, and sacrifice. His authority is marked by compassion. His commands are for our good. Because of that, we don't just obey; we *want* to obey. We see His love, and it makes us surrender joyfully.

The heart of this point is simple but life-changing: **Jesus deserves to rule your life, and He must be allowed to do so.** When we give Him that place, we don't lose freedom. We find it.

Do you think of Jesus more as your Savior or as your King? What would change if you gave Him "first place in everything"?

Jesus Does Not Rule By Intimidation

Many people initially turn to God because they're afraid—afraid of judgment, hell, or being lost. That fear can serve as a wake-up call. Scripture states it is a "fearful thing to fall into the hands of the living God" (Hebrews 10:31). However, fear alone isn't enough to sustain a lifetime of faithful service. Over time, fear can fade or change into guilt, resentment, or burnout. God never intended for fear to be the lasting foundation of our relationship with Him.

That's why Jesus doesn't lead through intimidation. He leads with grace. He rules not by forcing us into obedience but by inviting us into love. He will not govern your life through fear. He rules by invitation. His leadership is grounded in compassion, not coercion. He desires a willing heart, not a frightened one.

Yes, we need to show proper reverence for God. Scripture says He is to be feared (Psalm 96:4), and His justice is real (2 Thessalonians 1:7–9). But the gospel calls us to shift **from fear to faith**… moving from trembling before God's power to trusting in God's love.

Fear awakens. Love sustains.

That's what John clearly states: "There is no fear in love; instead, perfect love drives out fear, because fear involves punishment. So the one who fears is not complete in love," 1 John 4:18. Jesus desires more than just obedience; He seeks transformation. This transformation happens when we choose to follow Him out of love. As we deepen our relationship with Christ, our motivation should shift from avoiding punishment to joyfully pursuing Him. Fear might start the journey, but love must sustain it.

God does not force anyone to change. He waits patiently, speaks gently, calls us to grow, and gives us time. But He won't force us. The Spirit can be resisted (1 Thessalonians 5:19), and we can harden our hearts if we refuse to respond (Hebrews 3:15). That's why we must act now, not out of fear, but out of gratitude.

Have you ever tried to stay faithful to God mostly because you were afraid of what might happen if you didn't? What would it look like to serve Jesus out of love instead of fear?

Love Is the Only Lasting Motivation for Serving

Fear might get your attention, but it won't win your heart. True devotion isn't driven by fear; it's rooted in love. That's why, in the end, the only lasting reason to follow Jesus is love for Him.

John wrote: "We love because he first loved us," 1 John 4:19. When we truly grasp what Jesus has done for us—how He gave Himself completely and freely, rescued us from sin, and continues to serve us even now—our hearts are stirred. Service becomes a response to grace, not a reaction to fear. We don't serve Jesus to earn His favor; we serve Him because we already have it.

In the parable of the Good Samaritan (Luke 10:25–37), Jesus demonstrates what love looks like in action. The Samaritan didn't help the wounded man out of duty. He wasn't trying to earn righteousness. He acted out of compassion. He chose to do what was right because love motivated him. Jesus finished the story by saying, *"Go and do the same."*

That's the call for every citizen of the Kingdom. God doesn't desire empty actions. He seeks genuine love that leads to joyful obedience. Jesus said, *"If you love me, you will keep my commands"* (John 14:15). See the order: love first, obedience second. Obedience without love leads to legalism and pride. But love that flows out in obedience brings transformation.

"Without love, I am nothing," Paul said (1 Corinthians 13:2). We can attend every service, do all the right things, and still miss the heart of what it means to follow Jesus. We were created to love God, and that love must become our reason for everything we do.

What motivates your service to God right now … fear, guilt, habit, or love? How can you grow a deeper love that leads to joyful obedience?

Application: Choosing to Serve the King from the Heart

Serving Jesus is about surrendering to a King who gave everything for us. He doesn't demand our love; He invites it. He doesn't force us to obey;

He calls us to trust. And when we see what kind of King He is, the only right response is to give Him our whole heart.

We need to go beyond simple surface obedience. Jesus doesn't want people who serve out of guilt or fear. He desires those who understand His grace, people who see the cross, remember the empty tomb, and respond with grateful hearts. When we start to realize how much we have been loved, we begin to love in return. That love then shows in the way we speak, serve, forgive, and persevere when life gets tough.

The question isn't whether you are serving Jesus. The real question is *why*. Are you just going through the motions, hoping to stay on God's good side? Or are you serving out of joy, driven by love, and strengthened by grace?

Kingdom citizens don't serve because they have to. They serve because they want to. They've been rescued. They've been changed. And they now belong to a King who is worthy of everything.

So take a moment and ask yourself: What's driving my faith right now? What needs to change in my heart so that my service comes from love, not fear?

Conclusion

In a world where people fight for control, Jesus calls us to surrender. He is not a distant ruler demanding loyalty from a throne; He is the King who came close, laid down His life, and now invites us to follow Him freely. He doesn't rule through force or fear. He governs through love.

As members of His Kingdom, we must recognize this truth: **We are servants, but only because we choose to be.** Jesus won our hearts not through intimidation but through the cross. His kindness leads us to repentance. His sacrifice prompts us to obedience. His love becomes the foundation of everything we do.

Serving Christ isn't about fearing punishment or feeling pressured to perform. It's about knowing who He is, trusting what He has done, and willingly offering our lives to Him. That's true discipleship. And that's true joy in the Kingdom, when we set aside our pride, take our place as servants, and live each day under the good and gracious rule of our King.

For Discussion

Use the space below to reflect honestly on your relationship with Christ. Think not only about what you do, but *why* you do it.

1. Jesus has the right to rule your life. What does that look like practically in your daily decisions?

_____
_____
_____

2. In what ways might you be trying to "hold the throne" in your life instead of giving Jesus full control? What's keeping you from surrendering that area?

_____
_____
_____

3. Have you ever tried to serve God mostly out of fear or guilt? What helped (or could help) move your motivation toward love and gratitude?

_____
_____
_____

4. Jesus said, "If you love me, you will keep my commands" (John 14:15). What are some ways you can express love for Jesus through joyful obedience this week?

_____
_____
_____

5. Write down one truth or verse that encourages you to live with that mindset.

_____
_____
_____

Lesson 4

Daily Life in the Kingdom

And whatever you do, in word or deed, do everything in the name of the Lord Jesus, giving thanks to God the Father through him, Colossians 3:17

Introduction

It's easy to talk about serving Jesus during big moments, like Sundays, major decisions, or times of crisis. But what about the everyday? What does it mean to live as a citizen of God's Kingdom when you're doing laundry, sitting in traffic, attending school, or going to work?

One of the most powerful truths about the Kingdom of God is that it is not just a future promise, but a present way of life. When Jesus rules in your heart, **every moment matters**. The everyday becomes sacred. Daily life provides an opportunity to reflect the character of the King.

The Kingdom of God isn't limited to church buildings or religious events. It reaches into kitchens, classrooms, office meetings, hospital rooms, conversations with friends, and quiet moments alone. Kingdom citizens are not part-time Christians. We are dedicated full-time disciples. Our thoughts, words, and actions should mirror who we are, even when no one is watching.

That's why Paul wrote, *"Whatever you do, in word or in deed, do everything in the name of the Lord Jesus..."* (Colossians 3:17). That includes the routine, the unnoticed, and the small. In the Kingdom, even simple tasks become acts of worship when they are done with a heart submitted to Christ.

The Kingdom Shapes How We Think

Daily life in the Kingdom starts in the mind. Before your schedule is full, before you speak, before you act, your thoughts are already at work. What you allow into your heart and mind will influence how you live. That's why Kingdom living requires a different mindset.

Paul wrote in Romans 12:2: "Do not be conformed to this age, but be transformed by the renewing of your mind, so that you may discern what is the good, pleasing, and perfect will of God." The world constantly pressures us to conform, think as it does, value what it values, and pursue what it pursues. But Kingdom citizens aren't shaped by culture; Christ shapes us. We reject selfishness, pride, and shallow living. Instead, we fill our minds with truth. We think with humility. We pursue purity. We measure everything by the will of our King.

This mindset shift is not automatic. It takes intentional effort. That's why Scripture urges us to **focus on things above** (Colossians 3:2), to **take every thought captive to obey Christ** (2 Corinthians 10:5), and to **concentrate on what is true, honorable, and pure** (Philippians 4:8).

Living as a Kingdom citizen involves choosing what to focus on. It means filtering what you consume, including media, music, entertainment, and conversations. It also involves being aware of how certain thoughts influence your attitudes, emotions, and actions. Most importantly, it means submitting your thoughts to the King.

Because what controls your mind will ultimately influence your life.

What thoughts or habits are shaping your mindset right now? Are they leading you closer to the King, or pulling you away?

The Kingdom Shapes How We Speak

Words may seem small, but they reveal the heart and carry significant weight. In the Kingdom of God, our speech is not neutral; it either builds up or tears down. It either reflects the character of the King or mirrors the world around us.

Jesus said in Matthew 12:34: "For the mouth speaks from the overflow of the heart." In other words, what comes out of your mouth is a direct window into your soul. Angry words, gossip, harsh criticism, or crude jokes don't happen by accident. They reveal what's filling your heart.

Kingdom citizens are called to speak differently. Paul wrote in Ephesians 4:29: "No foul language should come from your mouth, but only what is good for building up someone in need, so that it gives grace to those who hear." That's the goal of Kingdom speech: **to give grace**. Whether you're talking with your spouse, a coworker, a stranger, or a child, your words hold power. Are they lifting someone up? Are they pointing people to Christ? Are they filled with truth and love?

This doesn't mean we shy away from tough conversations or speak without urgency. But it means we don't let anger, sarcasm, bitterness, or pride take control of our words. We allow Jesus to guide them.

Living in the Kingdom means thinking before we speak, speaking with purpose, and remembering that our words can either bring people closer to Jesus or push them away.

If someone recorded everything you said this past week, what would it reveal about who your King is?

The Kingdom Shapes How We Act

Kingdom citizenship isn't just about what we believe; it's about how we live. Faith that stays in the mind or heart but never shows in daily actions is incomplete. True allegiance to Jesus will always influence our behavior.

Paul talks about this in Colossians 3:12–14: "Therefore, as God's chosen ones, holy and dearly loved, put on compassion, kindness, humility, gentleness, and patience, bearing with one another and forgiving one another... Above all, put on love, which is the perfect bond of unity." These aren't just good ideas; they're daily choices and actions. Kingdom living shows in how we treat others, respond to inconvenience, handle conflict, and serve when no one is watching.

Consider your habits. How do you spend your time? How do you treat your family? How do you work and rest? All of it matters to Jesus. If He's your King, then every action becomes part of your worship.

James 1:22 reminds us: "But be doers of the word and not hearers only, deceiving yourselves." Kingdom citizens don't just know Scripture, they live it. They don't just talk about love, they demonstrate it. They don't wait for big moments to prove their faith; they consistently live faithfully in the small ones.

Every choice becomes a chance to show who your King is.

Are your daily actions aligned with Kingdom values, or just with what's comfortable or expected?

Application: Letting the King Shape Every Part of Life

Living in the Kingdom isn't about waiting for heaven; it's about following Jesus today, right where you are. When Christ is King, His rule influences everything. It impacts how you think, speak, and act, not just on Sundays, but every day.

The challenge isn't just understanding this; *it's actually practicing it*. Most people don't wake up each day intending to ignore Jesus, but it's easy to become distracted. It's simple to fall back into old habits—speaking carelessly, drifting into selfishness, worry, or laziness. That's why living in the Kingdom demands **deliberate effort**. You won't become a citizen of heaven by accident—you have to choose it every day.

Start small *by inviting Jesus into your morning routine*. Let His word shape your mindset before the world influences you. Ask Him to guide your words before you speak in conversations. Pause and pray before reacting to frustration or conflict. Make your home, your job, and your friendships everything where the King is honored.

Jesus doesn't want only part of your life; He desires the entire thing. When you live each moment under His rule, every daily moment becomes meaningful, and routine turns sacred. That's what life in the Kingdom looks like: Christ shaping everything.

Conclusion

The Kingdom of God isn't just a Sunday gathering or a future hope; it's a present reality for everyone who follows Jesus. If He is your King, then He must be Lord over every part of your life. That includes your thoughts, your speech, and your actions. Kingdom living isn't limited to big moments. It's reflected in the small decisions you make, such as what you say to your family, how you spend your time, and how you respond when things don't go your way.

Jesus calls us to live in a way that reflects His reign, not the culture around us. That means we don't let the world shape our mindset. We don't speak like everyone else. We don't act based on what's easiest or most popular. We let Christ shape our character every day.

Living this way takes effort and focus. However, it also brings peace, purpose, and joy. When we let the King lead every part of our lives, we discover what true freedom and faithfulness really mean.

The question to consider is simple: **Does my daily life reflect the Kingdom I claim to belong to?** If not, today is the perfect time to make a change, starting with the way you think, speak, and live.

For Discussion

Use the space below to reflect on how the rule of Christ shapes your everyday life.

1. What are some ways the world pressures you to conform in your thinking? *How can you renew your mind to reflect Kingdom values instead?*

_____
_____
_____

2. Think about your speech over the past few days. *Did the character of Christ shape your words? What would you like to change?*

_____
_____
_____

3. How does your daily routine reflect your citizenship in the Kingdom? *Where are you most consistent—and where are you most distracted?*

_____
_____
_____

4. Colossians 3:17 says to "do everything in the name of the Lord Jesus." *What would that look like in your home, workplace, or relationships?*

_____
_____
_____

5. What is one habit, attitude, or pattern of speech that needs to change so your life better reflects the reign of Jesus? *What will you do about it this week?*

_____
_____
_____

Lesson 5

The King's Job Plan

For we are his workmanship, created in Christ Jesus for good works, which God prepared ahead of time for us to do, Ephesians 2:10

Introduction

Every kingdom has tasks to complete. Citizens hold responsibilities. There are roles to fill, needs to meet, and purposes to achieve. But in Christ's Kingdom, the jobs aren't assigned based on status, wealth, or talent. They're given by grace, and they matter for eternity.

Too often, Christians see themselves as spectators. We assume that the "real work" belongs to preachers, elders, or missionaries. But Scripture teaches something very different. Every believer has been called into the King's service. Everyone has a job. Everyone has something to contribute. There are no bystanders in the Kingdom.

Paul wrote in Ephesians 4:12 that God gave leaders to the church "to equip the saints for the work of ministry." That word *ministry* isn't reserved for paid staff or public roles; it simply means service. If you're in Christ, you've been saved to serve. The King has a plan for you, and He expects you to live it out.

This lesson will help us realize that Kingdom work is about participation, not position. It's about faithfulness, not being seen. We'll understand that the Lord designed His body so that **every part matters**, and **each member has a mission**.

God doesn't just rescue us *from* something; He saves us *for* something greater. You have a role in His Kingdom, and whatever your job may be, it's not insignificant.

Every Citizen has a Role in the Kingdom

When you were baptized into Christ, you weren't just saved; you were enlisted. You became part of something bigger than yourself: the body of Christ. And in this body, **every part matters**.

Paul writes in 1 Corinthians 12:18–20:"But as it is, God has arranged each one of the parts in the body just as he wanted. And if they were all the same part, where would the body be? As it is, there are many parts, but one body." This truth challenges two common lies. One claims, *"I'm not needed."* The other claims, *"I don't need others."* Both are false. In Christ's Kingdom, no one is excluded, and no one stands alone. God has given each member a function, a gift, and a place. Whether your role is public or quiet, visible or behind the scenes, *it matters*.

The church is not a stage with just a few performers and many watchers. It's a living body, with every part working together. You might not preach or teach, but you could encourage, organize, repair, comfort, or show hospitality. Perhaps you pray faithfully or quietly support others. Don't underestimate the value of what you do.

Paul said in Romans 12:4–6: "Now as we have many parts in one body, and all the parts do not have the same function, in the same way we who are many are one body in Christ and individually members of one another. According to the grace given to us, we have different gifts…" You are not merely an audience member. You are a worker in the King's mission. The only question is whether you are doing your part.

Do you see yourself as an active part of the Kingdom, or more as an observer? What role has God placed in your hands?

Kingdom Work is About Faithfulness

In our world, success is measured by visibility … how many people notice you, how big your platform is, or how much praise you receive. But the Kingdom of God operates differently. The Lord doesn't reward popularity; He values **faithfulness**.

Jesus clearly illustrated this in the Parable of the Talents (Matthew 25:14–30). The master entrusted each servant with a different amount—one received five talents, another two, and the last one. Yet, in the end, the same words were spoken to the first two, despite their different returns.

"Well done, good and faithful servant." (v. 21)

Notice what truly mattered. Not the quantity, visibility, or size of the impact. What mattered was **faithfulness**. Did you use what you were given? Did you show up and serve? Were you steady, dependable, and willing to act?

This truth is both humbling and liberating. It means you don't have to do what someone else does. You don't have to be the most talented, the most educated, or the most experienced. You just have to be faithful. Show up. Do your part. Don't bury your gift.

Paul said in 1 Corinthians 4:2: "It is required that managers be found faithful." You may never stand before a crowd, but you can send an encouraging note. You might not travel overseas, but you can support someone who does. You may not teach a class, but you can demonstrate patience, kindness, and prayer in your home. Every act of service, done for the King, matters.

The Kingdom doesn't need superstars. It needs faithful servants.

> *Are you tempted to think your service doesn't matter because it's not seen? What would change if you truly believed that faithfulness is what God honors?*

God Prepares Us for the Work He Calls Us to Do

Serving in the Kingdom can feel overwhelming. You might ask yourself, *What do I have to offer?* or *Am I really equipped for this?* But Scripture reminds us that **God never calls us to serve without also preparing us for it.**

Look again at Ephesians 2:10: "For we are his workmanship, created in Christ Jesus for good works, which God prepared ahead of time for us to do." This verse tells us three things:

1. **You are God's workmanship**: you are not a mistake or an afterthought. You were intentionally shaped by the Creator.
2. **You were created for good works**: Your life has purpose. You are designed to serve, bless, build, and reflect the King.

3. **Those works were prepared for you**: God isn't improvising. He already has a plan for how your life can be useful in His Kingdom.

We often believe that only "qualified" people are useful to God. But Scripture challenges that view. God uses ordinary individuals—fishermen, tax collectors, shepherds, young women, widows, and former persecutors. What mattered wasn't their résumé. What mattered was their willing**ness to be used**.

You might not feel fully ready, but God equips you through His Spirit, His Word, and His people. He develops you through trials. He opens doors at the right time and gives you opportunities to grow.

The key is to be available. Open hands. Open heart. A willingness to say, "Here I am. Use me."

When the King gives you a job, He also gives you what you need to do it.

Have you been holding back because you feel unqualified or unsure? What would it look like to trust that God has already prepared you for His work?

Application: Step Into the Work God Has Given You

Kingdom work isn't just for a few; it's expected from everyone. If Jesus is your King, then you are His servant. You have a role. You might not have a title or the spotlight, but you have a calling. The question isn't whether you've been given a role — it's whether you're actually doing it.

This lesson reminds us that God doesn't require perfection or popularity. He asks for faithfulness instead. He simply wants us to show up, use what He has given us, and serve with a willing heart. That could mean helping behind the scenes, mentoring someone younger, encouraging the discouraged, or using your hands and time to meet a need. It might start small, but small actions matter in the Kingdom.

We also need to stop disqualifying ourselves. You don't need to be more talented, more confident, or more experienced. If God is your King, then He's already prepared you for the work He wants you to do. He knows your strengths and weaknesses. He knows where you're most effective. He doesn't make mistakes.

So what's holding you back? Are you waiting for permission? Seeking recognition? Paralyzed by fear? Let this be the moment you stop watching and start taking action. The King is calling. The Kingdom has work to do. And your role is crucial.

Conclusion

The Kingdom of God isn't made up of spectators. It is built by servants, ordinary people, doing their part in the work of the King. If you belong to Jesus, you have a job. You are part of His body. You've been gifted, placed, and prepared for a purpose.

This lesson reminds us that God's plan isn't about status or skill, it's about faithfulness. You don't have to do everything or be like someone else. But you are expected to do what God has given you to do. The only failure is doing nothing.

Jesus is not looking for perfection. He's looking for people who are willing. People who will say, "Here I am, Lord. Use me." The work may be small. It may be quiet. But nothing done for the King is wasted.

The Kingdom is growing. The mission is urgent. And the King is calling. Will you do your part?

For Discussion

Use this space to reflect on your role in God's Kingdom and how you can faithfully serve your King.

1. Read 1 Corinthians 12:18–20. *How does it change your perspective to know that God placed you in the body "just as He wanted"?*

_____
_____
_____

2. What lies or excuses have kept you from serving more fully in the Kingdom? *Where do you need to shift your mindset?*

_____
_____
_____

3. Think about the Parable of the Talents (Matthew 25:14–30). *What does it teach you about the importance of using what you've been given?*

_____
_____
_____

4. List one specific way God has gifted or prepared you to serve others. *How are you currently using that gift?*

_____
_____
_____

5. What is one action step you can take this week to step more fully into your Kingdom role? *Be specific.*

_____
_____
_____

Part Three

Listening and Obeying

Lesson 6

Citizens Listen to the King

My sheep hear my voice, I know them, and they follow me, John 10:27

Introduction

In any kingdom, the king's voice carries authority. His word is law. His commands are not questioned; they are obeyed. But in Christ's Kingdom, the king's voice is not only powerful but also personal. Jesus doesn't just issue commands; He speaks as a Shepherd who knows His people by name.

That's why listening is a clear sign of a Kingdom citizen. Jesus said, *"My sheep hear my voice, I know them, and they follow me"* (John 10:27). In this simple statement, Jesus explains what it means to belong to Him: we hear His voice and follow where He leads.

But listening isn't always easy. We live in a world filled with noise, news, opinions, distractions, and the pull of our own desires. It's easy to let those voices drown out the one voice that truly matters. And when that happens, we risk drifting away from the King we claim to follow.

This lesson is about tuning your heart to the voice of Jesus. It's about learning to recognize His words, respond to His teaching, and obey without hesitation. In the Kingdom, citizens don't just *know* what the King says, they listen carefully, and they do what He says.

Because in the end, the difference between hearing and doing is the difference between **a life built on rock** and **a life built on sand** (Matthew 7:24–27). True citizens listen, and their lives show it.

Jesus Expects His People to Hear and Obey

Jesus didn't speak just to be admired. He didn't teach for applause or attention. He spoke with authority, expecting His words to be **heard, believed, and obeyed**. In the Kingdom, listening is never passive. When the King speaks, His people respond.

At the end of the Sermon on the Mount, Jesus gave a powerful picture of what it means to truly listen. In Matthew 7:24, He says: "Therefore, everyone who hears these words of mine and acts on them will be like a wise man who built his house on the rock."

Hearing without action is not enough. A few verses later, Jesus warned that many will call Him "Lord, Lord," but not enter the Kingdom, because they **did not do** the will of the Father (Matthew 7:21). The danger isn't in failing to hear, it's in failing to obey.

God has always tied listening to obedience. In the Old Testament, Israel was told repeatedly: *"Hear, O Israel…"* But their downfall came when they stopped listening … when they heard the words but hardened their hearts (see Jeremiah 7:23–24).

The same danger exists today. We can grow familiar with the Bible. We can nod in agreement during sermons. However, if we don't obey and **act**, we are not truly listening.

Kingdom citizens don't just know the King's words. They live them.

Is there any area where you've been hearing Jesus, but not responding with action? What needs to change?

We Learn to Hear His Voice Through the Word

In a world filled with noise, how do we know what Jesus is saying? How do we recognize His voice?

Jesus does not speak to us today through visions or whispers in the wind. He speaks through His **Word**, the living, powerful, inspired Scriptures. If you want to hear the voice of the King, open your Bible. That's where His voice is heard most clearly.

Paul reminds us in 2 Timothy 3:16–17: "All Scripture is inspired by God and is profitable for teaching, for rebuking, for correcting, for training in righteousness, so that the man of God may be complete, equipped for every good work." Scripture is not just a book of advice. It is the voice of God in written form. It's how He teaches, corrects, guides, and equips us. That means reading the Bible is not a religious habit—it's a relational act. It's how we listen to our King.

But many Christians struggle with this. Some only open their Bible on Sundays. Others get discouraged because they don't always understand what they read. But like any relationship, hearing God's voice takes time, effort, and consistency.

The more you immerse yourself in His Word, the more clearly you begin to hear Him. You start to recognize His tone, His priorities, and His commands. His words begin to shape your thinking, your desires, and your choices.

To the Colossians Paul said: "Let the word of Christ dwell richly among you, in all wisdom teaching and admonishing one another through psalms, hymns, and spiritual songs, singing to God with gratitude in your hearts," Colossians 3:17. If you want to follow the King, you have to know what He says. And if you want to know what He says, you have to spend time in His Word.

Are you regularly listening to the voice of the King through Scripture—or are other voices louder in your life?

Listening Leads to Trust and Obedience

True listening goes beyond just hearing. It builds **trust**, and trust leads to **obedience**. This is what sets Kingdom citizens apart from casual believers. They don't just hear the King's words—they put their lives on the line for them. They obey even when it's difficult, even when it costs something, because they trust that the King is good.

In Luke 5:4–5, we see a clear example with Peter: "When he had finished speaking, he said to Simon, 'Put out into deep water and let down your nets for a catch.'
'Master,' Simon replied, 'we've worked hard all night long and caught nothing. But if you say so, I'll let down the nets.'" Peter didn't understand why, but he obeyed. Why? Because **Jesus said so**. That's what trust looks like. He had heard enough from Jesus to believe that His words could be trusted.

Listening like that requires humility. It means we admit we don't always know best. It means we submit, even when it goes against our instincts or preferences. It means we choose to obey—not because it always makes sense, but because we know **who** is speaking.

Jesus said in **John 14:15**: "If you love me, you will keep my commands." That's the heartbeat of the Kingdom. Real love listens. Real love obeys. Citizens of the Kingdom don't follow perfectly, but they follow sincerely. They learn to trust the King more and more as they hear His voice and respond with faith.

Is your life showing that you trust Jesus enough to do what He says—even when it's hard or inconvenient?

Application: Listening Leads to Action

Listening to Jesus is more than reading your Bible or nodding along to a sermon. It's about **aligning your life** with the voice of the King. It means letting His words carry more weight than the world's. It means acting on what you hear—not just agreeing with it.

Every day, you are listening to someone. News, social media, opinions, emotions, and habits are shaping you. But Jesus says, *"My sheep hear my voice."* That means you must be intentional. You must make room to listen. You must quiet the noise and open the Word. You must train your heart to respond to His leading.

And when He speaks, you must act. Obedience is where faith becomes real. The Kingdom belongs to those who not only **hear** the words of Jesus but also **build** their lives on them. That may mean forgiving someone who hurt you. Speaking kindly when you'd rather lash out. Staying faithful when it would be easier to quit. These are not just moral decisions. They are Kingdom responses to the King's voice.

So, ask yourself: **Am I truly listening?** And if so, what am I doing with what I hear?

Conclusion

In Christ's Kingdom, listening is not optional; it's essential. The King has spoken, and His citizens are known by their response. Jesus made it simple: *"My sheep hear my voice… and they follow me."* That's the pattern of Kingdom life: **hearing and following**.

But listening isn't just about knowing Scripture. It's about obeying it. It's about letting God's Word shape your choices, your attitude, and your priorities. It's about submitting your will to His. True Kingdom citizens trust their King enough to do what He says, even when it's difficult or unpopular.

This lesson reminds us that the strength of your faith is not measured by how much you've heard—but by how much you've done with what you've heard. Because in the end, only one foundation will stand: the one built on hearing and obeying the words of Jesus.

Tune your heart to the voice of the King. Open His Word. Listen carefully. And then … follow.

For Discussion

Use these questions to examine how well you are hearing, and responding to, the voice of your King.

1. Jesus said, "My sheep hear my voice... and they follow me" (John 10:27). *What does this verse mean to you personally?*

_____
_____
_____

2. Think about your current Bible habits. *How regularly are you listening to the King through His Word?* **3. Is there a command or teaching from Jesus that you've been hearing but not obeying?** *What's been holding you back?*

_____
_____
_____

4. What are some practical ways you can tune out the world's noise and better hear Jesus this week?

_____
_____
_____

5. Describe a time when you listened to Jesus and obeyed—even when it was hard. *What was the result?*

_____
_____
_____

Lesson 7

Three Attitudes Kingdom Citizens Must Avoid

For everyone who exalts himself will be humbled, but the one who humbles himself will be exalted, Luke 18:14

Introduction

The Kingdom of God is not just about what we do, it's about who we are on the inside: our mindset, our motivations, our attitudes. Jesus never just focused on outward behavior. He exposed what was going on in the heart because the heart reveals where our loyalty really lies.

Throughout His teaching, Jesus constantly challenged attitudes that had no place in His Kingdom: pride, hypocrisy, resentment, self-righteousness, greed, and indifference. These weren't just minor flaws; they were serious warning signs that someone did not truly understand the heart of the King.

In Luke 18, Jesus shared a parable about two men who went to pray. One was confident in his own righteousness, while the other simply said, *"God, have mercy on me, a sinner."* Only one of them left justified. The message was clear: **you can't bring a spirit of pride or superiority into the presence of a holy God.**

This lesson will challenge us to examine our hearts and identify attitudes that hinder our growth and harm our witness. It's not just about avoiding certain behaviors … it's about allowing Jesus to reshape how we think and how we treat others.

In the Kingdom, pride is replaced by humility. Bitterness is replaced by grace. Self-focus is replaced by service. And those who belong to the King must learn to recognize and reject anything that doesn't reflect His heart.

Pride: Trusting In Yourself Instead of the King

Pride is one of the most destructive attitudes in the Kingdom, and one of the easiest to hide. It's the belief that we're doing fine on our own, that we've earned our standing before God, or that we're better than others who struggle.

Jesus exposed this attitude in the parable of the Pharisee and the tax collector (Luke 18:9–14). He told the story "to some who trusted in themselves that they were righteous and looked down on everyone else." The Pharisee stood proudly, listing off all the good things he had done. The tax collector stood at a distance, wouldn't even look up, and prayed for mercy.

And Jesus said the humble man, the one who knew he had nothing to offer, went home justified.

Pride is not just arrogance. It's **self-reliance**. It shows up when we act like we don't need grace, when we measure ourselves by others, or when we quietly think God should be impressed with us. But pride blinds us to our sin. It keeps us from repentance. And worst of all, it pushes us away from the King who gives grace to the humble.

James 4:6 says: "God resists the proud but gives grace to the humble." In the Kingdom, pride has no place. Citizens of the King know they are what they are **only by His grace** (1 Corinthians 15:10). That awareness influences how they treat others and how they walk with God—never boasting, always relying on Him.

Where do you see signs of pride in your thinking, words, or prayers? What would it look like to truly depend on God instead of yourself?

Bitterness: Holding On to Offense Instead of Extending Grace

Bitterness might not always be visible on the outside, but it corrupts the heart. It develops quietly, nourished by hurt, resentment, disappointment, or anger. And if left unchecked, it snuffs out love, hinders forgiveness, and destroys unity. That's why bitterness has no place in the life of someone who follows the King.

In the Kingdom, grace is the standard. Jesus tells a powerful story in Matthew 18:21–35 about a servant whose master forgave an unpayable debt. But that same servant went out and violently demanded repayment from someone who owed him just a little. When the master found out, he was furious. Why? Because **those who receive mercy are expected to show mercy.**

Bitterness arises when we forget how much we've been forgiven. It occurs when we replay the wrongs done to us but overlook the mercy God has shown us. The longer we cling to the offense, the less space we have for grace.

Paul warned the church in Ephesians 4:31–32: "Let all bitterness, anger and wrath, shouting and slander be removed from you, along with all malice. And be kind and compassionate to one another, forgiving one another, just as God also forgave you in Christ." The Kingdom is a place of healing, not hostility. Of release, not revenge. Kingdom citizens don't deny pain, but they refuse to let it define them. They trust the King with justice, and they choose to walk in the same grace they've received.

Is there someone you haven't truly forgiven? How is holding on to bitterness affecting your walk with Christ?

Self-Centeredness: Living for Your Agenda Instead of the King's

One of the biggest challenges in the Kingdom is learning that life is not about you. The world teaches us to prioritize comfort, convenience, and personal success. But Jesus calls His followers to die to self, take up their cross, and follow Him. That's a radical shift, and it confronts every form of self-centeredness.

In Luke 9:23, Jesus said: "If anyone wants to follow after me, let him deny himself, take up his cross daily, and follow me." This is not a call to part-time discipleship. It's a call for complete surrender. Kingdom citizens are not focused on building their platform, protecting their preferences, or controlling outcomes. They seek first the Kingdom (Matthew 6:33), not their comfort first.

Self-centeredness can be subtle. It appears in how we spend our time, how we treat others, and how we respond when things don't go our way. It causes resentment when service goes unnoticed or when others don't meet our expectations. It keeps us focused on what we're missing rather than what we've been given to share.

But the Kingdom is not about getting your way; it's about yielding to the King. When Jesus reigns, our priorities shift. We stop asking, *"What do I want?"* and start asking, *"What does He want?"*

Paul modeled this mindset in Galatians 2:20: "I have been crucified with Christ, and I no longer live, but Christ lives in me …" That's the heart of Kingdom living. The throne belongs to Jesus, not to us.

In what ways are you still trying to keep control of your life instead of yielding fully to Christ?

Application: Watch Your Heart—Because Attitude Shapes Everything

In the Kingdom, your attitude is just as important as your actions. You might say the right things and still feel pride. You can serve visibly and still hold onto bitterness. You can attend worship but spend the rest of the week focused only on yourself. When these attitudes take hold, they distort your relationship with the King, and with others.

That's why Jesus spent so much time revealing the heart. He didn't want followers who just went through the motions. He desired citizens who were humble, merciful, and surrendered. That kind of life doesn't happen by accident. You must **watch your heart**. You need to examine your motives. You should invite God to search you, break down what doesn't belong, and renew your spirit.

The good news is this: these attitudes can be changed. Pride can be replaced with humility. Bitterness can be healed by grace. Self-centeredness can give way to surrender. But that only happens when we come to the King honestly and let His Word do its work in us.

So don't just ask, *"What am I doing?"* ask, *"Who am I becoming?"* Because in the Kingdom, your attitude is one of the clearest signs of who really rules your life.

Conclusion

Being a citizen of the Kingdom isn't just about outward obedience; it's about inner transformation. Jesus isn't only shaping what we do; he's reshaping how we think, how we feel, and how we treat others. That means confronting attitudes that shouldn't be in His Kingdom.

Pride, bitterness, and self-centeredness are not harmless flaws. They serve as barriers to growth. They hinder our fellowship with God and harm our influence with others. They reveal a heart that has not been fully surrendered to the King.

But Jesus doesn't just point out what's wrong. He offers a better way. He invites us to live in humility, extend grace, and prioritize His purposes over our own. When we do, we reflect the heart of the King, and we make His Kingdom visible through our lives.

The challenge is simple: don't just manage your behavior. Examine your attitude and ask the Lord to remove anything that doesn't reflect Him. Because in the Kingdom, your heart matters.

For Discussion

Use these questions to reflect on your heart and the attitudes that shape your life in the Kingdom.

1. Read Luke 18:9–14. *Why was the tax collector justified instead of the Pharisee? What does this teach you about pride?*

_____
_____
_____

2. Bitterness is often hidden. *Are you holding on to hurt, resentment, or unforgiveness in any area of your life?*

_____
_____
_____

3. What signs of self-centeredness can you identify in your daily priorities or choices? *How does this compare with Jesus' call to deny yourself?*

_____
_____
_____

4. What practical steps can help you replace pride with humility, bitterness with grace, or self-focus with surrender? *Be specific.*

_____
_____
_____

5. Pray and ask God to reveal one attitude He wants to change in you. *Write your prayer or your response to what He shows you.*

_____
_____
_____

Lesson 8

Kingdom Citizens Focus on Heaven

So if you have been raised with Christ, seek the things above, where Christ is, seated at the right hand of God. Set your mind on things above, not on earthly things, Colossians 3:1–2

Introduction

Where you focus determines how you live. If your attention is always on the present, on money, comfort, success, or control, you'll live as if this world is all there is. But if your eyes are fixed on something bigger, your values and decisions start to shift.

Kingdom citizens are called to see things differently. Our eyes aren't focused on earth; they are lifted toward heaven. Not because we're trying to escape, but because we understand where our true home is. Paul told the Colossians, *"Set your minds on things above, not on earthly things."* Why? Because we've been raised with Christ. Our lives are now hidden in Him. And one day, we will appear with Him in glory (Colossians 3:1–4).

This is a clear call to live with a Kingdom mindset. It involves making choices based on eternal truths rather than temporary gains. We don't chase what the world pursues. We don't fear what the world fears. We live with hope, purpose, and direction that come from heaven, not from the culture around us.

This lesson prompts us to consider where our attention truly is. Are we merely living as strangers passing through, or as people who have made this world our home? Jesus warned that it's possible to gain the whole world and still lose your soul. But citizens of the Kingdom keep their eyes on the King—and on the home He's prepared for them.

We Live as Strangers and Exiles on the Earth

One of the key truths about Kingdom life is that this world is not our home. As followers of Christ, we are called to live with the mindset of

pilgrims, people who are passing through, not settling in. That means our hopes, our treasures, and our identity must be rooted somewhere beyond this life.

Hebrews 11 speaks of the faithful men and women who lived by faith, even though they didn't receive everything God promised in their lifetime. Hebrews 11:13 says: "They confessed that they were foreigners and temporary residents on the earth."

They understood something we often forget: if we belong to a heavenly Kingdom, we might not always feel at home here. Our values won't always match the world's. Our direction may seem unfamiliar. Our choices will often stand out. And that's exactly how it should be.

Peter taught on this in 1 Peter 2:11: "Dear friends, I urge you as strangers and exiles to abstain from sinful desires that wage war against the soul." When you forget that you're just passing through, it becomes easy to compromise. You start to build your life around comfort, achievement, or acceptance. Instead of trying to fit in, you should stand apart. But Kingdom citizens know they're not called to blend in; they're called to be faithful.

Living with heaven in view means we hold the things of earth loosely. We're grateful for what God provides, but we don't let possessions, popularity, or position define us. Our hearts belong elsewhere. We're living for a better country, a heavenly one (Hebrews 11:16).

Do you live like a temporary resident, or more like someone settling in for good? What would change if you truly believed this world is not your home?

Our Focus Shapes Our Desires and Decisions

What we focus our minds on shapes who we become. That's why Scripture tells us not just to believe in Christ, but to **focus** on Him. Because when your eyes are fixed on heaven, your choices on earth start to reflect your eternal priorities.

Take notice of Paul's words in Colossians 3:2: "Set your minds on things above, not on earthly things." This is more than a call to think about heaven occasionally. It's about daily direction. The word *set* means to anchor or fix your thoughts, like a compass pointed north. It's a mindset that says, *"What matters most is not what I gain here, but what honors Christ."*

That kind of focus changes what you love, how you spend your time, how you handle temptation, and how you face suffering. It keeps you from being consumed by worry or greed. It frees you from chasing approval. It gives you peace when life doesn't make sense because you're grounded in something bigger than this life.

The opposite is also true. If your focus is on things like wealth, comfort, power, or appearance, your life will mirror those values. You'll make choices based on short-term gains instead of long-term faithfulness. You'll live with urgency for the wrong things and miss out on the joy of what truly lasts.

Jesus warned in Matthew 6:21: "For where your treasure is, there your heart will be also." Kingdom citizens store up treasure in heaven. That's not just about giving, it's about longing for what lasts. It's about wanting more of Christ and less of everything else.

What are your current priorities revealing about your focus? Are your daily decisions shaped more by eternity, or by what's convenient or comfortable right now?

Hope in Heaven Gives Us Strength to Endure Now

Focusing on heaven doesn't mean ignoring the struggles of earth, it means enduring them with hope. Kingdom citizens are not spared from pain, loss, or difficulty. But they face it differently. They know that what is coming is greater than what is happening.

Paul reminds us of this in 2 Corinthians 4:16–18: "Therefore we do not give up. Even though our outer person is being destroyed, our inner person is being renewed day by day. For our momentary light affliction is producing for us an absolutely incomparable eternal weight of glory. So we do not focus on what is seen, but on what is unseen. For what is seen is temporary, but what is unseen is eternal."

This is how the early Christians kept going when they were misunderstood, persecuted, or suffering. They didn't lose heart. They looked beyond what was visible and focused on what lasts forever.

Hope in heaven brings clarity amid chaos. It reminds us that suffering is not the end. It helps us resist trading eternal reward for temporary relief. It strengthens our resolve when obedience costs us something. And it allows us to wait confidently, knowing the King is returning, and His reward is with Him (Revelation 22:12).

This world can wear you down. But the promise of heaven lifts your eyes. It doesn't erase the pain, but it gives purpose to it. Kingdom citizens walk through this life knowing where they're headed, and that hope shapes everything.

How does the promise of eternal glory help you face challenges today? Are you letting hope shape your endurance?

Application: Keep Your Eyes on What Lasts

Where you fix your eyes will shape your life. If you stay focused on what is temporary, you'll live for fleeting things. But if your mind is set on things above, you'll begin making decisions that reflect your true citizenship. That means saying no to sin, holding loosely to possessions, and being willing to stand out for your faith because you know this world is not your home.

This kind of mindset requires discipline. The world constantly pulls your attention downward and tempts you to chase what's urgent instead of what's eternal. That's why you must keep reminding yourself of who you are and where you're headed. You belong to the King, and your home is with Him. Everything you do now—how you serve, how you suffer, how you speak—should point to that reality.

When life feels heavy, look up. When decisions become difficult, think eternally. When you're tired or discouraged, recall the promises of your King. He hasn't forgotten you. He's preparing a place for you, and He's coming back.

So don't let the world define you. Don't let comfort distract you. Keep your focus on what lasts. Because Kingdom citizens are people of eternal focus and unshakable hope.

Conclusion

To live in the Kingdom is to live with your eyes fixed beyond this world. Kingdom citizens know they don't fully belong here. They live as strangers and exiles, grateful for God's blessings on earth, but longing for what is to come. Their decisions, their values, and their endurance are all shaped by the reality of heaven.

This kind of focus doesn't come naturally. It requires faith. It means choosing to believe that unseen things are more real than what we can touch. It means seeking Christ above all else and resisting the pull of a world that runs in the opposite direction.

But the reward is worth it. The path may be narrow and the road may be hard, but those who stay focused on the King and His promises will not be disappointed. Their hope is sure. Their future is secure. And their lives, even now, reflect the light of the world to come.

So lift your eyes. Live with heaven in view. And remember: this world is not your home.

For Reflection

Use these questions to check your focus and renew your hope as a citizen of heaven.

1. Read Colossians 3:1–2. *What does it mean to "seek the things above"? How does that show up in your daily life?*

_____
_____
_____

2. Hebrews 11:13 says God's people confessed they were "foreigners and temporary residents." *Do you live with that kind of mindset, or do you feel too at home in this world?*

_____
_____
_____

3. What are some earthly things that compete for your attention and pull your focus off of Christ?

_____
_____
_____

4. Read 2 Corinthians 4:16–18. *How can this passage help you endure trials or disappointments in life?*

_____
_____
_____

5. What is one habit or mindset you could begin this week to help fix your eyes more intentionally on heaven? *Be specific.*

_____
_____
_____

Part Four

Our Identity and Mission

LESSON 9

What It Means to Be a Citizen

Our citizenship is in heaven, and we eagerly await for a Savior from there, the Lord Jesus Christ, Philippians 3:20.

Introduction

Everyone belongs somewhere. We carry IDs, passports, and addresses that tell the world where our home is and whose authority we live under. But for those who follow Jesus, our most important identity isn't tied to a nation or an earthly place. It's found in this truth: **"Our citizenship is in heaven"** (Philippians 3:20).

That statement isn't just about our future home; it's about our present allegiance. If we belong to Christ, then we already live under His rule. We are citizens of a Kingdom that is not of this world. This influences how we think, act, speak, and treat others. It means our loyalty does not primarily lie with culture, politics, or tradition, but with the King.

In the Roman world, citizenship came with rights and responsibilities. It provided protection, but it also demanded obedience. Similarly, our heavenly citizenship is both a privilege and a calling. We have been rescued by grace, but now we are expected to live in a way that reflects the values of our King.

This lesson looks at what it really means to be a citizen of heaven. It's more than just claiming a spiritual identity. It's about living a way of life that reflects the heart of Jesus, right now, in a world that desperately needs to see it.

Citizenship Means Belonging to a Kingdom and a King

When Paul says in Philippians 3:20, *"Our citizenship is in heaven,"* he's not talking about where we'll go someday; he's talking about where our **allegiance already belongs**. To be a citizen of heaven means we belong to a real Kingdom, ruled by a real King: Jesus Christ.

In the Roman world, citizenship was everything. It determined your legal status, your rights, and your protection. Paul himself used his Roman citizenship to avoid unlawful punishment (Acts 22:25–29). But here in Philippians, he highlights something much more important. As believers, we are **not primarily citizens of any earthly nation**. We are citizens of the Kingdom of God.

Jesus declared in John 18:36: "My kingdom is not of this world." His Kingdom is eternal, spiritual, and just. It doesn't fluctuate with politics. It isn't limited by borders. And it requires our utmost loyalty. That means our values are guided by His Word, not public opinion. Our behavior follows His commands, not personal preference. And our ultimate hope rests in Him, not in any human system.

Citizenship means you live under the authority of the King. You accept His rule. You represent His reign. And you never forget who you belong to.

Do you live as someone who belongs to Jesus above all else? What would others learn about your citizenship by watching your life?

Citizenship Comes With a New Way of Life

Being a citizen of heaven isn't just about believing something different; it's about living differently. The values of the Kingdom are not optional; they are the expectations of life under Christ's rule.

Paul emphasizes this in Philippians 1:27: "Just one thing: As citizens of heaven, live your life worthy of the gospel of Christ." The word "worthy" doesn't mean we earn our salvation. It means we live in a way that reflects the gospel we believe. In other words, if Jesus truly rescued us, changed us, and brought us into His Kingdom, then our actions should show it. Kingdom citizens don't just speak differently; they love differently, forgive differently, serve differently, and suffer differently.

This new life involves how we treat others, how we utilize our time, how we manage hardship, and how we cope with temptation. It influences every part of who we are. And it's not shaped by culture or comfort, it's shaped by the King.

Titus 2:11–12 reinforces this: "For the grace of God has appeared, bringing salvation for all people, instructing us to deny godlessness and worldly lusts and to live in a sensible, righteous, and godly way in the present age." Kingdom citizens live on earth as people whose lives are anchored in heaven. Their conduct gives the watching world a glimpse of what it looks like when Jesus reigns.

Does your daily life reflect the values of heaven or the patterns of this world? What area needs to come more fully under the rule of Christ?

Citizenship Carries a Mission to Represent the King

Kingdom citizens are not just called to live differently, they are called to **represent** the King wherever they go. Citizenship isn't private. It's public. It means we are ambassadors of Christ, sent into the world to reflect His character, share His message, and advance His cause.

Paul explains this in 2 Corinthians 5:20: "Therefore, we are ambassadors for Christ, since God is making his appeal through us. We plead on Christ's behalf: 'Be reconciled to God.'" Ambassadors don't speak for themselves. They speak on behalf of the one who sent them. In the same way, citizens of the Kingdom are sent to represent Jesus in how they speak, serve, love, and lead. Your job, your neighborhood, your school, your social circles, these are the places where the King is known through your life.

This responsibility isn't limited to evangelism. It includes integrity, compassion, humility, and courage. When the world sees you respond to pressure, temptation, injustice, or disappointment, they should see the difference that Jesus makes.

Philippians 2:15 puts it this way: "...so that you may be blameless and pure, children of God who are faultless in a crooked and perverted generation, among whom you shine like stars in the world." That's the calling of a citizen: to shine in a dark world, not to draw attention to ourselves, but to point people to the King we serve.

Where has God placed you to represent Him? How can you more clearly reflect the King in your words and actions?

Application: Live Like You Belong to the King

Citizenship shapes identity. It reveals where your loyalty lies and how you act in the world. If your citizenship is in heaven, then your life should mirror the character, priorities, and mission of the King. That means every day—at home, work, church, in public, and in private—you're showing the world who rules your life.

It's easy to forget this. It's easy to blend in, to prioritize convenience, or to seek approval from others. But Kingdom citizens are called to something greater. We don't live by the world's standards; we live by the values of the gospel. We show compassion when others show anger. We live with truth and grace when the culture calls for compromise. We forgive when others hold grudges. We love even when it's not returned. That's the life of someone who belongs to Jesus.

But citizenship also brings hope. We recognize that our Savior is coming. Until then, we live as if we are already home. We act as if His reign is happening now—because it is. Our task is to make that reign visible to the world.

So walk with purpose. Speak with boldness. Love with humility. And let your life show it: **You belong to the King.**

Conclusion

Being a citizen of heaven isn't just a future promise; it's a present identity. When you were brought into the Kingdom of God, everything changed. You came under the rule of a new King. You received a new way of life, and you were entrusted with a mission: to represent Christ in the world.

This lesson reminds us that citizenship involves both privilege and responsibility. We are saved by grace, but we are also called to live in a way that reflects that grace. Our lives should mirror the King we serve. Our words should communicate the hope of the gospel. And our priorities should clearly reveal where our true home is.

The world needs to see what it looks like when Jesus reigns in someone's heart. And God has chosen you to show them.

So live like you belong. Stand out for the right reasons. Shine like a light in a dark world. And never forget: your citizenship is in heaven, and your King is coming.

For Discussion

Use these questions to reflect on how your life shows your loyalty to the King.

1. Read Philippians 3:20. *What does it mean to you personally that your citizenship is in heaven?*

_____
_____
_____

2. Paul says in Philippians 1:27 to "live your life worthy of the gospel of Christ." *In what areas of your life are you doing that well? In what areas do you struggle?*

_____
_____
_____

3. How does being a Kingdom citizen shape your attitude toward culture, politics, or personal goals?

_____
_____
_____

4. In what ways can you better represent Christ as His ambassador this week? *Be specific about where and how.*

_____
_____
_____

5. Think about someone in your life who doesn't know Jesus. *What would they learn about your King by watching your life?*

_____
_____
_____

Lesson 10

Forgiveness in the Kingdom

For if you forgive others their offenses, your heavenly Father will forgive you as well. But if you don't forgive others, your Father will not forgive your offenses, Matthew 6:14–15.

Introduction

Forgiveness isn't just a Christian virtue; it's a requirement of the Kingdom. In the world, forgiveness is often optional, delayed, or withheld. But in the Kingdom of God, it's expected. Why? Because every citizen of the Kingdom has been forgiven far more than they will ever be asked to forgive.

Jesus made this clear when He taught His disciples to pray: *"Forgive us our debts, as we also have forgiven our debtors"* (Matthew 6:12). Then He followed up with a warning: if you withhold forgiveness, don't expect to receive it. That's not because God is cruel. It's because **refusing to forgive shows a heart that hasn't truly understood grace**.

The Kingdom is founded on mercy. At the core of our faith is a King who bled for His enemies, prayed for His executioners, and bore the burden of our sin so we could be set free. To follow that King is to demonstrate that mercy. And to reject forgiveness is to reject the very foundation of the gospel.

This lesson will examine what forgiveness looks like, why it's important, and how we can live it out even when it's challenging. Because in the Kingdom, forgiveness isn't just a command … it's a way of life.

Kingdom Citizens Forgive Because They've Been Forgiven

The foundation for forgiveness in the Kingdom is not how badly we've been hurt. It's how deeply we've been forgiven. We don't extend grace because people deserve it, we extend grace because we didn't.

In Ephesians 4:32, Paul writes: "And be kind and compassionate to one another, forgiving one another, just as God also forgave you in Christ." This is the pattern: God forgave you, now you forgive others. The mercy you've received becomes the mercy you give. That's what makes the Kingdom different from the world. In the world, people hold grudges. They demand payback. They use past offenses as weapons. But in the Kingdom, citizens let go, not because the hurt wasn't real, but because the cross was.

In the parable of the unmerciful servant (Matthew 18:21–35), Jesus tells of a man who was forgiven an enormous debt but refused to forgive someone who owed him a small amount. The message is clear: **when we refuse to forgive, we show that we've forgotten the mercy God showed us.**

Forgiveness doesn't mean forgetting or pretending the pain didn't happen. It means releasing the offense and entrusting justice to God. It means choosing mercy over resentment, not once, but often.

Do you truly believe that God has forgiven you completely? How is that belief shaping the way you treat those who've hurt you?

Forgiveness is Not Optional

Jesus didn't present forgiveness as an option. He made it a requirement for Kingdom life. If we want to receive mercy from the King, we must be willing to extend it to others.

In Matthew 6:14–15, Jesus said: "For if you forgive others their offenses, your heavenly Father will forgive you as well. But if you don't forgive others, your Father will not forgive your offenses." This is a strong warning. It shows that forgiveness is not just a personal choice; it's a spiritual requirement. You can't live under God's grace while refusing to extend that grace to someone else.

This doesn't mean forgiveness is easy. Some wounds are deep, and some betrayals take time to heal. But Jesus never said forgiveness was simple, He said it was necessary. When we hold back forgiveness, we stiffen our hearts, becoming prisoners of bitterness, and we lose touch with God's mercy.

Forgiveness isn't about fairness, it's about freedom. It's not excusing sin, it's releasing its grip on your heart. And in the Kingdom, **forgiven people forgive**. That's the pattern. That's the calling.

Is there someone you're still refusing to forgive? What is that doing to your relationship with God?

Forgiveness Sets You Free

Forgiveness is not just a command, it's a gift. It sets you free. When you forgive, you're no longer defined by what someone did to you. You're no longer stuck in a cycle of anger, bitterness, or resentment. You are free to walk in the grace and peace that comes from God.

Paul describes this new way of life in Romans 12:17-19: "Do not repay anyone evil for evil. Give careful thought to do what is honorable in everyone's eyes. If possible, as far as it depends on you, live at peace with everyone. Friends, do not avenge yourselves; instead, leave room for God's wrath..." Forgiveness doesn't mean justice doesn't matter. It means we trust God with the outcome. It means we surrender the right to get even, and we allow God to handle wrongs in His perfect way. That's what frees us, not just from others' sin, but from our own cycle of pain.

When you forgive, you don't forget what happened. Instead, you release it. You stop carrying it around. You create space for healing and peace. And you live like someone who truly belongs to the Kingdom. Forgiveness is how grace flows. It's how the Kingdom grows. It's how people see the heart of Jesus through your life.

Are you holding on to something that's keeping you stuck in anger or hurt? What would it look like to release it into God's hands today?

Application: Forgiven People Forgive

Forgiveness is a clear sign that we truly understand the gospel. When we forgive others, we're not just showing kindness; we're demonstrating that we've been changed. We mirror the character of a King who forgave us at great cost, even while we were still sinners.

In the Kingdom, forgiveness isn't based on how we feel. It's an act of obedience and trust. We choose to forgive even when it's difficult. Even when the pain still lingers. Even when the other person doesn't apologize. Why? Because God forgave us. Because the cross is enough. And because we don't want anything to block our relationship with the Lord.

Forgiveness is not a sign of weakness; it's a sign of strength. It takes courage to let go of your right to revenge. It takes faith to trust God with justice. And it takes love to move forward without holding a grudge. But when you forgive, you open space for healing, freedom, and peace. You release the grip of bitterness and step into the grace that defines the Kingdom.

So if you've been holding onto something, let it go. If you've been wronged, release it. If you've wronged someone else, go make it right. In the Kingdom, we don't keep score. We extend grace because we know what it means to be forgiven.

Conclusion

Forgiveness isn't just a part of Kingdom life; it's at its core. Every citizen of the Kingdom lives under the mercy of the King. We were rescued not because we earned it, but because Jesus paid our debt in full. That grace defines us, and it's what we are called to extend to others.

When we refuse to forgive, we undermine the very foundation of our faith. But when we forgive, we reflect the King. We show the world that grace is real, that mercy is stronger than revenge, and that healing is possible.

This lesson reminds us that forgiveness is both a responsibility and a gift. It frees us from bitterness. It draws us closer to God. And it puts the gospel on display.

If you belong to Jesus, you are a forgiven person. So live like it. Speak like it. And forgive like it. Because in the Kingdom, forgiveness is not optional; it's the way of life.

For Discussion

Use these questions to examine your heart and walk more fully in the mercy of the King.

1. Read Matthew 6:14–15. *What does this passage reveal about the seriousness of forgiveness in the life of a Christian?*

_____
_____
_____

2. Think about the mercy God has shown you. *How does remembering your own forgiveness help you forgive others?*

_____
_____
_____

3. Is there someone you are struggling to forgive? *What is keeping you from releasing that offense to God?*

_____
_____
_____

4. What do you think forgiveness is, and what is it not? *How do those beliefs shape the way you respond when you've been hurt?*

_____
_____
_____

5. What step can you take this week to live out forgiveness, either by releasing a grudge or seeking reconciliation?

_____
_____
_____

Lesson 11

Ambassadors of the Kingdom

Therefore, we are ambassadors for Christ, since God is making His appeal through us. We please of Christ's behalf: "Be reconciled to God.",
2 Corinthians 5:20.

Introduction

Every kingdom sends out ambassadors, people who represent it and carry its mission into distant places. In the same way, every citizen of God's Kingdom has been given a role that is far greater than personal comfort or private beliefs. We are **ambassadors of the King.**

Paul says in 2 Corinthians 5:20, *"We are ambassadors for Christ, since God is making his appeal through us."* That's a staggering thought. The God of heaven chooses to speak through **His people**. He invites us to represent Him, to live and speak in ways that reflect His grace, truth, and authority.

Being an ambassador means we don't live for ourselves. We live on assignment. We carry a message that doesn't belong to us. We represent a Kingdom that isn't visible to the world but is real, powerful, and coming in fullness. And through us, the King calls people to Himself.

This lesson encourages us to see ourselves not only as saved but also as **sent**. Not just as believers, but as **messengers**. Because in the Kingdom of God, every citizen is called to be a representative, and every moment presents an opportunity to make the King known.

Ambassadors Represent the King, Not Themselves

An ambassador never speaks for themselves. Their job is to speak on behalf of the one who sent them. They don't get to change the message. They don't push their personal agenda. Their task is simple: **represent the King with clarity, loyalty, and honor.**

That's exactly what Paul states about us in 2 Corinthians 5:20: "We are ambassadors for Christ, since God is making his appeal through us." As citizens of the Kingdom, we don't just deliver a message; we carry the **authority and purpose** of the King. Every conversation, decision, and relationship becomes a place where we either reflect Christ, or we don't.

This is a serious responsibility. It means people are watching our actions. They observe how we handle conflicts, how we communicate online, how we serve others, and how we respond under pressure. And throughout it all, we're representing Jesus, whether we intend to or not.

Jesus said in Matthew 5:16: "Let your light shine before others, so that they may see your good works and give glory to your Father in heaven." We don't shine for our own name. We shine for His. That's what it means to be an ambassador. Your life is a witness. Your words carry weight. You are not here for yourself; you are here for Him.

What kind of picture are you giving others of Jesus? Does your life point people to the King—or to something else?

Ambassadors Carry the Message of Reconciliation

Every ambassador has a message to share. For those in the Kingdom of God, that message is clear: **"Be reconciled to God."** That's what the King wants the world to hear, and He has entrusted that message to His people.

Paul writes in 2 Corinthians 5:18–19: "Everything is from God, who has reconciled us to himself through Christ and has given us the ministry of reconciliation… and he has committed the message of reconciliation to us." Reconciliation means restoring peace where there was separation. Sin created a divide between God and humanity. But Jesus stepped in, bore our guilt, and made peace through His blood. Now, we're not only forgiven, we're sent. We're given the responsibility to share that message with others.

That doesn't mean we save people. But it does mean we speak. We listen. We reach. We care. We invite. We share the gospel, not as experts, but as people who have been rescued and want others to know the way home.

This is personal. You know people who are still far from God. You cross paths every week with neighbors, coworkers, friends, and even family members who don't yet know what Jesus has done for them. As an ambassador, you're not just living near them, you're sent **to** them.

God has placed His message in your hands. Don't keep it to yourself.

Who in your life needs to hear the message of reconciliation? What's stopping you from sharing it?

Ambassadors Live with Purpose, Not Passivity

Ambassadors don't drift; they are intentional. They understand they are on assignment and live accordingly. That's the calling for every citizen of the Kingdom: to live with clarity, courage, and purpose—not just on Sundays but in every part of life.

Paul describes this mission-minded life in 2 Timothy 2:4: "No one serving as a soldier gets entangled in the concerns of civilian life; he seeks to please the commanding officer." Ambassadors stay focused. They don't get distracted. They don't let cultural values steer them off track. They remember why they're here and who they're serving.

Too often, Christians live as if they've been rescued but not given a mission. But the truth is, if you belong to the King, you've been called to **represent Him every day**. That includes your workplace, your home, your conversations, your priorities, and your plans. You are here on purpose, for the sake of others and to bring glory to God.

Jesus said in John 20:21: "As the Father has sent me, I also send you. This is not just for preachers or missionaries. It's for every Kingdom citizen. The King has sent you. So live like it. Speak like it. Walk through every day knowing your life matters, not because of what you accomplish, but because of **who you represent.**

Are you living each day as someone sent by God, or have you settled into spiritual autopilot?

For Application: Step Into Your Calling

If you're a citizen of the Kingdom, you're not just saved; you're sent. God didn't rescue you so you could remain idle. He made you an ambassador—someone who carries the message of His grace into a world full of brokenness and confusion.

This is now your identity. You speak for the King. You represent His heart. You demonstrate His mercy and truth through your life. That means every moment counts. Every relationship matters. Your words carry significance. You're not waiting for a special opportunity; you're already on a mission.

You don't need to be loud or perfect. You just need to be faithful. Be kind when others are harsh. Be honest when others distort the truth. Be bold when it's easier to stay quiet. Let people see Jesus in how you respond, serve, and speak. And when the opportunity arises, share the message that changed your life: **Be reconciled to God.**

This world needs ambassadors who are alert, willing, and unashamed. The King is reaching out to others through you. So step into your calling and represent Him well.

Conclusion

Being an ambassador isn't just a side role; it's at the core of our identity as citizens of the Kingdom. God has trusted us with His message and His mission. He sends us into the world to speak on His behalf and to mirror His character.

This calling is not about being perfect. It's about being faithful, faithful to the truth, to love, and to living and speaking in a way that points people to Jesus. You no longer represent just yourself; you represent the King.

Let this lesson serve as a reminder: your life is not random. Your presence in your family, workplace, or community is not by chance. You are on a mission. You are here for a purpose. The King is reaching out to others through you.

For Discussion

Use these questions to reflect on how you are representing your King in everyday life.

1. Read 2 Corinthians 5:20. *What does it mean to you that God is "making His appeal through us"? How seriously do you take that role?*

_____
_____
_____

2. Think about how you live at work, at home, and online. *Do your actions reflect the character of Christ? What needs to change?*

_____
_____
_____

3. Who in your life needs to hear the message of reconciliation? *What would it look like for you to be an ambassador to them?*

_____
_____
_____

4. Read John 20:21. *Jesus said, "As the Father has sent me, I also send you." What does that mean for how you approach daily life?*

_____
_____
_____

5. What distractions or fears keep you from living with Kingdom purpose? *How can you move forward with greater clarity and courage?*

_____
_____
_____

PART FIVE

Faithful Until He Comes

Lesson 12

Kingdom Stewardship: Using Our Gifts for God's Glory

Just as each one of you has received a gift, use it to serve others, as good stewards of the varied grace of God, 1 Peter 4:10.

Introduction

In the Kingdom of God, nothing truly belongs to us. Our time, talents, resources, and opportunities all come from the King. Because they come from Him, they are not just blessings to enjoy; they are responsibilities to manage. That's what stewardship means: recognizing that everything we have belongs to God and using it in ways that honor Him.

Too often, we think of stewardship only in terms of money. But biblical stewardship is much broader. It's about how we use our gifts, how we serve others, how we show hospitality, how we give our energy, and how we invest our lives. It's about using whatever God has placed in our hands to reflect His grace and to advance His Kingdom.

Peter writes, *"Just as each one has received a gift, use it to serve others, as good stewards of the varied grace of God"* (1 Peter 4:10). That means no one is left out. Every citizen of the Kingdom has something to offer. And no gift is too small to matter. What matters is faithfulness.

This lesson will challenge you to view your life as a trust from God. You have been equipped, called, and placed for a purpose. The question is: are you using what He's given for His glory, or are you keeping it for yourself?

Everything We Have is From God

The foundation of stewardship is humility. We must realize that **nothing we have truly belongs to us.** *Everything,* our abilities, opportunities, resources, and influence, is a gift from God. He is the Giver, and we are the managers.

James 1:17 reminds us: "Every good and perfect gift is from above, coming down from the Father of lights, who does not change like shifting shadows." This means your skills are not random. Your position is not accidental. Your blessings are not earned. Everything good in your life is a trust from the King. And with that trust comes responsibility.

In the parable of the talents (Matthew 25:14–30), Jesus describes a master who trusts his servants with different amounts of silver while he is away. The faithful servants invest and multiply what they are given. The unfaithful servant buries his gift out of fear and laziness. When the master returns, each one gives an account, not for what they didn't have, but for what they did.

That's how it works in the Kingdom. God doesn't expect you to do everything, but He does expect you to do **something** with what He's given you.

Do you see your time, gifts, and resources as yours—or as tools God has entrusted to you for His purpose?

Every Gift Has a Purpose in the Kingdom

God doesn't give gifts at random. He gives them on purpose, for a reason. And that reason is never self-promotion or self-preservation. In the Kingdom, gifts are meant to serve. They're given so others can be strengthened, encouraged, helped, and pointed to Christ.

Peter puts it plainly in 1 Peter 4:10: "Just as each one has received a gift, use it to serve others, as good stewards of the varied grace of God." Notice the language: *each one has received a gift*. That includes you. No one is left out. You may not have a stage or a spotlight, but your gift matters. Whether it's teaching, encouraging, organizing, listening, showing hospitality, leading, creating, or giving, God intends to use it in His Kingdom.

Paul also covers this in Romans 12:6: "According to the grace given to us, we have different gifts…" The variety of gifts shows the richness of God's grace. No two believers are exactly alike, but each one plays a part in the body of Christ. When we all use our gifts, the church becomes stronger. Needs are met. People are built up. And God is glorified.

The opposite is also true. When we hide our gifts or only use them for ourselves, others suffer. The work slows down, and the mission is delayed. That's why stewardship matters.

What gifts has God given you, and how are you using them to serve others in the Kingdom? What's being left unused?

Faithful Stewards Glorify God, Not Themselves

In the Kingdom, success is not measured by how much we've been given, but by how **faithfully** we use it. Some are entrusted with visible gifts. Others serve behind the scenes. But in the end, what matters is not attention or applause. What matters is whether God is glorified.

Peter continues in 1 Peter 4:11: "If anyone speaks, let it be as one who speaks God's words; if anyone serves, let it be from the strength God provides, so that God may be glorified through Jesus Christ in everything." That's the goal: **that God may be glorified in everything**. Our gifts are not about building our reputation. They're about reflecting the goodness of the Giver. When we speak, serve, lead, give, or teach, it's not to draw attention to ourselves. It's to point people to Jesus.

Faithful stewards don't compete or compare. They concentrate on being trustworthy with what they've been entrusted with. Regardless of whether your role is big or small, public or private, God notices your faithfulness. He is pleased when you use what He has given you to bless others and honor Him.

Jesus said in Luke 16:10: "Whoever is faithful in very little is also faithful in much…" So don't wait for more. Be faithful with what you have now. Because in the Kingdom, even the smallest act done in Jesus' name brings glory to God.

Are you using your gifts to honor God, or to build your own comfort, image, or influence? What would it look like to serve with no need for recognition?

Conclusion

In the Kingdom of God, everything we possess is a gift, and each gift is a responsibility. We are not owners, but caretakers. What we have received is not for our comfort, status, or control. It is for God's glory and the well-being of others.

This lesson reminds us that faithful stewardship is not optional for Kingdom citizens. It's part of our identity. God has equipped each of us with unique abilities, resources, and opportunities. What matters is not how much we've received, but whether we're using it well.

The world urges us to make a name for ourselves. The King calls us to establish His. When we serve openly, with humble hearts and a focus on His glory, our lives become part of something eternal.

So take what God has placed in your hands, whatever it is, and use it. Because in the Kingdom, nothing given to God is ever wasted.

For Discussion

Use these questions to reflect on how you're managing what God has entrusted to you.

1. Read 1 Peter 4:10. *What does this verse teach about the purpose of your gifts?*

_____
_____
_____

2. Make a list of your strengths, talents, or resources. *How are you currently using these in service to others?*

_____
_____
_____

3. Read the parable of the talents in Matthew 25:14–30. *Which servant do you most relate to—and why?*

_____
_____
_____

4. Are there gifts or opportunities God has given you that are currently being unused? *What is holding you back from putting them to work?*

_____
_____
_____

5. What is one step you can take this week to use your gifts more intentionally for God's glory?

_____
_____
_____

Lesson 13

Until the King Comes: Holding Fast in the Kingdom

He called ten of his servants, gave them ten minas, and told them, "Engage in business until I come back," Luke 19:13.

Introduction

Every citizen of the Kingdom exists in a space between two great realities: the reign of Christ that has already begun, and the return of Christ that is still to come. We live in the tension of the "already" and the "not yet." The King has come, defeated sin, and claimed His throne. But He has not yet returned to judge the world and completely establish His Kingdom. So what are His people supposed to do in the meantime?

Jesus answers that question through the Parable of the Minas (Luke 19:11–27). The story tells of a nobleman who goes away to receive a kingdom. Before leaving, he entrusts resources to his servants and tells them, *"Engage in business until I come back."* That one command captures the main point of this final lesson: **stay faithful, stay active, and stay ready until the King returns.**

Kingdom citizens do not wait passively. We are not meant to just sit still or merely get by. Instead, we are called to live with purpose, courage, and endurance. We are called to work, watch, and hold firm to the mission given to us. When the King comes, He will call His people to account, not for how much they achieved, but for whether they remained faithful.

This final lesson concludes the quarter with a simple yet powerful question: *Are you still holding on tightly?* Not just in belief, but in obedience, service, and hope. Because the King is coming, and He expects His people to be prepared.

The King Has Entrusted Us with a Mission

Jesus' parable in Luke 19 shows us something clear: when the King left, He didn't leave us empty-handed. He gave His servants something to work with, and a responsibility to fulfill. He expects His people to live with purpose and courage until He comes again.

In Luke 19:13, the nobleman says: "Engage in business until I come back." That wasn't a suggestion; it was a command. Every servant was expected to take what had been given and do something with it. Not for their own benefit, but for the King's. And that's still the call for every citizen of the Kingdom today.

We are not waiting idly; we are living on a mission. The gospel has been entrusted to us. The Spirit has been given to equip us. The Word has been provided to lead us. And the world surrounds us, full of people who need to know the King.

The question isn't, "Do I have a role?" The question is, "Am I using what the King gave me?" Every resource, opportunity, and conversation, these are the minas the King has trusted to you. He wants His work to progress while He is away. And when He comes back, He will ask what we did with what we had.

What has the King placed in your hands? Are you actively engaged in His mission—or waiting on the sidelines?

Faithfulness is Proven Over Time

The parable in Luke 19 spans a long period. The nobleman departs to receive his kingdom, and **"after he returned, having received the kingdom, he summoned those servants"** (Luke 19:15). That time between his departure and return is where we currently live—and it's the period in which true faithfulness is tested.

Anyone can serve for a season. Anyone can be bold when the moment feels exciting. But kingdom faithfulness is about long-term commitment. It persists even when things are tough, even when results are slow, and even when the King seems distant. The test isn't how quickly you act, it's how **steadily** you endure.

This is why **Hebrews 10:23** tells us: "Let us hold on to the confession of our hope without wavering, since he who promised is faithful." God hasn't called us to flashy results. He's called us to steady obedience. To live with integrity, serve when no one sees, and keep sowing even if we don't yet see the harvest. The faithful servants in Jesus' story didn't all produce the same results, but they all used what they had. That's what pleased the King.

There will be times you're tired, discouraged, or wondering if your work matters. But remember: the King sees. And He honors those who **hold fast** and keep working until He returns.

Are you tempted to give up, slow down, or drift in your service to the King? What helps you stay grounded in long-term faithfulness?

The King Will Return and Set Things Right

The parable of the minas ends with a moment of judgment. The nobleman returns, not just to see what his servants have accomplished, but to **settle accounts**. Those who were faithful are rewarded, while the lazy or rebellious face loss. The message is clear: **the King is returning, and what we do now matters.**

Jesus says in Luke 19:15: "At his return, having received the kingdom, he summoned those servants he had given the money to, so he could find out how much they had made in business." This is a reflection of reality. One day, Christ will return. The waiting will end. And every citizen of His Kingdom will stand before Him, not to be condemned but to give an account of how they lived. For the faithful, this will be a moment of joy. For the careless, a moment of regret.

2 Corinthians 5:10 says: "For we must all appear before the judgment seat of Christ, so that each may be repaid for what he has done in the body, whether good or evil." This emphasizes the urgency of our faith. It reminds us that time is limited and the mission is real. But it also offers hope, because when the King returns, He will make everything right. Every wrong will be judged. Every faithful act will be remembered. And every burden carried for Him will be worth it.

Does the return of Christ give shape to the way you live each day? How would your focus change if you remembered daily that the King is coming?

For Application

The message of this final lesson is simple but urgent. The King is returning. In the meantime, He has given you a calling. You're not here to coast. You're here to **live faithfully**, keep serving, loving, building, and working for the good of the Kingdom.

You don't have to do everything, but you are responsible for what God has entrusted to you. The people in your life, the resources you've received, and the truths you understand—all of it is part of your calling. Every day presents a chance to act as a true citizen of the Kingdom.

Waiting isn't easy. There are distractions, discouragements, and setbacks. But none of that changes the truth: the King will return. And when He does, what will matter is not your status or success, but your faithfulness. Did you hold fast to His Word? Did you stay committed to His work? Did you live in a way that showed the world whose you are?

Hold fast. Stay ready. Keep going. The King is coming.

Conclusion

The story of the Kingdom doesn't end when the King leaves; it ends when the King returns. Until that day arrives, every citizen has a responsibility. We are not just spectators; we are stewards. Our task is clear: be faithful with what we've been given, live intentionally, and hold firmly to our hope.

This lesson and this quarter remind us that the Kingdom is not a distant idea. It is our present reality and our future hope. We have been called, equipped, and sent. And the time we've been given is not for drifting, but for devotion.

As you finish this study, ask yourself: Am I still holding firm? Am I living like someone who belongs to the King? Am I using what He's given me for His glory?

The King is coming. Let Him find you faithful.

For Discussion

Use these questions to reflect on your faithfulness, focus, and readiness as a citizen of the Kingdom.

1. Read Luke 19:13. *What does it mean to "engage in business until I come"?*

_____
_____
_____

2. What specific things has God entrusted to you (gifts, opportunities, people, responsibilities)? *Are you actively using them for His purposes?*

_____
_____
_____

3. How do you stay faithful when you feel tired, discouraged, or uncertain about your impact? *What has helped you keep going in hard seasons?*

_____
_____
_____

4. Read 2 Corinthians 5:10. *How does the reality of standing before Christ one day influence your choices today?*

_____
_____
_____

5. If Jesus returned this week, what would you want Him to find you doing? *What can you change or commit to in order to live with that kind of readiness?*

_____
_____
_____

www.ingramcontent.com/pod-product-compliance
Lightning Source LLC
LaVergne TN
LVHW010319070426
835510LV00031B/3451